COOKING WHAT COMES NATURALLY

COOKING WHAT

COMES NATURALLY

*A Natural Foods Cookbook
Featuring a Month's Worth of
Natural-Vegetarian Menus*

NIKKI GOLDBECK

Illustrated by Bill Goldsmith

DOUBLEDAY & COMPANY, INC.
GARDEN CITY, NEW YORK
1972

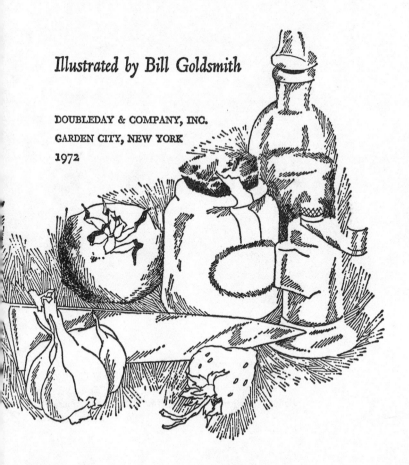

FOR DAVID

CONTENTS

INTRODUCTION

This is a book for people who want to eat better. It is a manual for those who recognize that many of the products on the market today, developed in the interest of convenience, have been over-processed, overseasoned, and so well preserved that this convenience has replaced the nutritional purpose food is meant to serve.

There are chemical additions to almost every commercial food item. All are of undetermined, but possible, toxicity. Many are added for esthetic reasons—they make food more attractive; others make the food easier to handle, more palatable with the least amount of work, and simpler to store. They do not contribute to the life sustaining value of the food. Your health is a high price to pay for these qualities.

In certain areas industry has stepped in and taken complete control of the available food supply. This is true of meat and poultry production. Most meat on the market today comes from animals raised in carefully controlled, artificial environments. They are fed chemically treated, highly processed foods and are injected with hormones to fatten them up, making their flesh an undesirable source of nourishment.

Many people have decided to reject the empty foods which have been forced on them by intensive advertising and promotion. To do this an alternative must be found for those foods which have been highly tampered with.

There is an alternative. If you are interested in eating foods that are good for you—foods with a natural, richer taste—and are uncertain how to go about it, here is your guideline.

This book has been developed in the interest of a different kind of convenience—to make sound, healthy eating as simple as it really is.

The heart of this book is a series of vegetarian menus which provide a nutritionally sound basis for you to begin—one for each day of the month. They are meals built around fresh fruits and vegetables, whole grain cereals and cereal products, natural seasonings, and unrefined sweeteners. There is nothing artificial about these foods. These are substantial, honest, everyday meals.

In addition, these pages teach you to prepare a wide variety of tasty, satisfying dishes, buy foods that are good for you, and plan exciting meals based on these foods.

Your biggest surprise will come in finding how creative natural-vegetarian dishes can be. You'll be dining on casseroles, stews, cutlets, and crepes; favorite foods from South America to the Middle East. The rich taste of fresh, natural ingredients combined with the variety of unique dishes you will now be able to prepare, will keep you cooking what comes naturally.

I

Natural Food and
What It's All About

VARIETY ON THE TABLE

Undoubtedly you already have a number of dishes you regularly prepare which fall into the category of natural foods. Many other recipes are commonly available in all cookbooks. Keep these in mind for creating your own menus. Consult general and foreign cookbooks for these supplementary recipes, especially the sections on vegetables, salads, and soups. Recipes can often be altered to accommodate your needs by substituting fresh fruits and vegetables for canned, using vegetable stock rather than meat stock or bouillon, and making use of whole grain flour, "raw" sugar, and honey to replace their counterparts. Hints for making these changes are given in the chapter on Ingredient Substitutions. Adjustments in seasoning to taste may be needed. Altering recipes for baked products is tricky and requires some trial and error.

The recipes given in the menu section will add some new and exciting dishes to your repertoire. Many of them require some advance planning—marinating cold salads for 1 or 2 days, soaking beans before cooking them, or in some cases additional time on the day you wish to use them—making home-baked breads and homemade tomato sauce. As suggested when they appear on the menu, homemade breads and tomato sauce can be prepared in quantity at any time and stored in the freezer for future use. This is also true of a number of other dishes as indicated in the recipes.

In a pinch use canned beans cooked in salt and water only (check the label). Your local health food store offers some very tempting alternatives to homemade breads and desserts.

Try to give your meal some forethought. If it's the night before, splendid—you'll have plenty of time to do any preparation. If this is inconvenient, try taking this book with you to work, school, or on your daily rounds. Before you head for home decide what you would like for dinner. That way you can pick up any additional ingredients you may need to carry out the recipe. You'll soon get into a convenient pattern and will find cooking a creative and enjoyable pastime.

Remember: The menus here are only a guideline. They are as flexible as you are.

AN ADEQUATE DIET

Many friends ask how they can be certain they are getting adequate amounts of the essential nutrients.

The human body has many functions to perform daily. The process of living involves continual wearing out and replacing of body cells. In order to accomplish this the body has certain nutritional requirements.

Energy is needed to power these changes. Carbohydrates and fats are the primary sources of this energy. Carbohydrates are digested quickly for immediate energy while fats are digested slowly and provide satiety so you are not hungry soon after you have eaten. In addition, fats and carbohydrates are used for giving warmth and creating protective fat to maintain this warmth and cushion nerves and muscles.

Protein is needed by the body to build and repair cells for tissues and muscles; to promote growth and maintain the body in a healthy state. Extreme fatigue is one symptom of insufficient protein. Most American diets provide an overabundance of protein to the extent of 20 to 25 percent above the figure recommended as adequate. This is not to say every American is well supplied with protein since lack of information and resources leaves the diets of many deficient in all nutrients. When there is an excess of protein it is used to provide energy along with the carbohydrates and fats. Because protein foods are the most costly they are an unnecessarily expensive source of energy.

Minerals are needed in conjunction with proteins to aid tissue growth, particularly in the bones, teeth, blood, and nervous system.

Vitamins are essential in the diet to help regulate body processes. They do not take part directly in the building or energy-giving process.

A healthy diet consists of adequate amounts of all these nutrients. A balanced meal is one which contains foods rich in protein, minerals, vitamins, quick and slow fuel, plus roughage and water for proper digestion.

All foods contain some energy, referred to as calories. Sugar and starch are the main sources. The skin and stalks of fruits and vegetables, and the bran, or outer coating of grain, are the best roughage. Obtaining sufficient amounts of energy foods and roughage presents no special problem for the vegetarian. Our main concern here is with adequate amounts of protein, minerals, and vitamins.

A healthy diet does not limit itself to good food at one meal each day . . . it encompasses a total life style in which every meal (and everything else you eat and drink) is important for its contribution to the daily food intake. This applies to any eating pattern you may follow. The most efficient way to achieve good health is for each meal to be balanced.

To be sure you are receiving enough protein, vitamins, and minerals it is important to learn what foods are good sources of each. There are so many variables in each food item it is virtually impossible to give exact food values without chemical analysis. Foods do fall into categories, though, and a wide selection from each category is your assurance your diet is a healthy one.

In planning your meals and snacks include some of the foods listed in each of the groups below and your diet will be rich in all the essentials.

Protein Foods: Because meat and fish have become the primary sources of protein in our culture the vegetarian is often concerned about the source of protein in the diet. The following foods are all good sources of protein:

eggs; milk, milk drinks, and yoghurt; cheese, nuts, and nut butters (especially peanut butter); sunflower and sesame seeds; dried peas and beans, especially lentils, soy beans, chick peas, kidney beans, and lima beans; bean sprouts; dried figs and dates; whole grain flours and cereals including whole wheat flour, corn meal, corn flour, cracked wheat, wheat germ, unhulled barley, unhulled (brown) rice, and oats; and, to some extent, plant roots, leaves, and seeds. For this reason plenty of fresh chopped parsley, celery tops, and other vegetable tops are excellent additions to salad.

Vegetable and cereal protein may be low in certain amino acids, particularly lysine. Cheese and milk protein exhibit a relative surplus of lysine and are therefore valuable supplements to vegetable protein. Foods that contain incomplete proteins can be combined to create excellent sources of complete protein.

Since whole grains are an important source of protein in a vegetarian diet it is very important to use whole grain baked products instead of white breads and bakery goods.

Minerals: Calcium is important for strong teeth and bones, muscles, and nerves. These foods are all good sources of this mineral: sunflower and sesame seeds; pistachio nuts; Brazil nuts; filberts; almonds; dried figs and dates; leafy green vegetables; dried peas and beans; milk; cheese; egg yolk; molasses.

Iron is needed for healthy blood. Iron deficiency, a cause of anemia and extreme sluggishness, is all too common in the American diet. It can be avoided by eating: dried fruit; raisins; molasses; dried beans; spinach; egg yolks; brown rice; nuts.

Phosphorus works in conjunction with calcium for strong bones, teeth, muscles and nerves. It is found in: cheese; egg yolk; chocolate; dried beans and peas; nuts; whole grains.

Iodine is necessary for proper functioning of the thyroid gland. Sea salt is an excellent source.

Vitamins: Fruits and vegetables are the primary source of vitamins and all make some contribution in this area. The vegetarian should have little difficulty obtaining all the necessary vitamins. Other foods also rich in vitamins are included in the following list along with the most plentiful plant sources.

Vitamin A is essential for clear skin, good vision, and resisting infection. Most green leafy vegetables (especially dark outer leaves) and yellow or orange fruits and vegetables are excellent sources of vitamin A, particularly: spinach; broccoli; carrots; sweet potatoes; pumpkin; winter squash; cantaloupe; apricots; egg yolks; milk fat; butter; cream; and, yellow corn meal.

The Vitamin B Complex consists of a number of vitamins among which niacin, thiamin, and riboflavin are the most well known. A lack of these vitamins is often the cause of skin disorders. They are also important for digestion of protein and proper elimination. The B vitamins are removed in the milling process used to make white flour, and as a result products made with white flour are low in B vitamins. The specific vitamins which make up the complex and their sources include:

Thiamin—whole grains, especially whole wheat; nuts; dried peas and beans; brewer's yeast; sunflower and sesame seeds; potatoes; brown rice; oatmeal.

Riboflavin—green leafy vegetables; dried beans and peas; milk; eggs; brewer's yeast.

Niacin—whole grains; dried beans and peas; mushrooms.

Pantothenic Acid—whole grains, especially whole wheat; wheat germ; brewer's yeast; peanuts; mushrooms; dried peas and beans; molasses; eggs.

Vitamin B-6—wheat germ; seeds; egg yolks; leafy greens.

Folacin and B-12—green leafy vegetables; milk, yoghurt; eggs; cheese. Those who consume no animal biproducts may have difficulty getting enough B-12 and should take a supplement.

Vitamin C is another essential vitamin. It cannot be stored in quantity in the body and supplies must be replenished regularly. It is an important vitamin for resistance to infection, strengthening blood vessels, healing of wounds and keeping gums healthy. The vitamin is easily destroyed in foods by exposure to light, heat, chopping, long storage and it is soluble (therefore easily lost) in liquid. Raw fruits and vegetables are the best sources, including: citrus fruits, such as oranges and grapefruits; strawberries and wild berries (and well prepared berry jams); cabbage; green pepper; broccoli; cauliflower; tomatoes; potatoes; Brussels sprouts.

Vitamin D is called the "sunshine vitamin" and it affects all glandular functions. Being outdoors is the best source since your body has the ability to convert ultraviolet light from the sun's rays to vitamin D.

Other vitamins, also essential but less well known and understood are supplied by proper intake of those vitamins just listed.

Generally speaking, foods are best eaten in the whole, unprocessed, natural state. Fruits, vegetables, nuts, and seeds are best nutritionally (and also tastiest) eaten raw.

All foods should be chewed thoroughly to a smooth consistency to be properly digested. Food which is not digested cannot be assimilated into the body and the goodness it provides will be lost.

It takes very little effort to increase the nutritional content of your meals. Some quick additions to already familiar dishes include:

1. Use liquids in which dried beans and vegetables are cooked as bases for soups and sauces.

2. Add leftover, cold, cooked beans to salads.

3. Sprinkle chopped nuts, sunflower seeds, or grated cheese on salads and sauces.

4. Chopped nuts are delicious in sandwich spreads; perfect with cream cheese on whole grain bread.

5. Peanut butter and fresh banana or pear slices make great sandwiches.

6. Do not remove parsley used for flavor in cooking. Instead of a sprig of parsley on the side of the plate as a garnish, chop it and use it in eggs, soup, salad, and vegetable casseroles. Ironically, this rich source of nutrients is usually discarded or ignored.

7. Fresh lemon juice enhances flavor and vitamin content of salads and fresh fruits.

8. Include a teaspoon or two of grated orange or lemon rind in puddings and when baking. A natural flavoring agent.

9. Add fresh or dried fruits to cereals, puddings, and baked goods.

10. Add wheat germ when baking; sprinkle it on cereals; mix it with flour or crumbs for breading and toppings.

11. A little fat (butter or cream) in cereal or on bread satisfies you longer than dry bread or plain cereal.

12. Add a few tablespoons dry milk powder to cooked cereal; to the milk used on dry cereal; to the flour when baking.

SHOPPING FOR FOOD

As a general rule, foods that are the closest to their natural state are the best for you. The basic tenets which follow will help you choose the foods best suited to your needs.

Due to the widespread destruction of the environment some form of contamination exists in all food products. The idea is not to over react and reject all available foods, but at the same time not to accept the harm that is being done as irreversible. The most effective approach comes in selecting those foods which have been minimally effected, increasing the market for these products and encouraging food processers to become more conscientious and responsive to our demands.

The term "natural," as it is used here, refers to foods available in the native, unprocessed state, or foods prepared without the addition of artificial flavors, colors, chemicals, or highly processed foods among the ingredients.

The term "organic" refers to the way in which the food has been raised—in a natural setting free from chemical feed, pesticides, and herbicides.

The goal of natural food cooking is to combine foods in the native state into enjoyable meals, eliminating all artificial additives from the diet. Natural cooking can be accomplished whether or not the food source is raised organically, but the final dishes will be much tastier and totally chemically free if organic produce is used. The ultimate end is, therefore, natural foods organically raised.

Most of the products mentioned here are available in health food stores. With the increasing awareness of the dangers of processed foods, more and more health food stores are opening around the country. These stores specialize in organically grown products and unadulterated foods. This does not mean there are no intentional or unintentional misrepresentations of food on their shelves or that everything sold in health food stores is good for you. Your own awareness will be your best guide.

A number of organic food outlets ship their stock anywhere in the country to stores and individuals. For a list of shipping houses and stores in your area consult *Prevention Magazine*. While I don't endorse many of their contentions, the magazine does a fine job in this area. Also, a booklet published by Rodale Press—*Guide to Organic Foods Shopping and Organic Living*—is an excellent resource book. In addition, more and more of these items are appearing on the shelves of local supermarkets and food stores. Hopefully, as the demand increases, this trend will continue.

Meat: As previously stated, most meat that is marketed today comes from animals raised specifically to be consumed. These animals are raised in carefully controlled environments, fed chemically treated and synthetically enriched foods, and injected with artificial hormones to fatten them up. These hormones bring about chemical alteration in the animal, change the metabolism and lead to weight gain—a gain of fat and water which is nutritionally insignificant. Any of these hormones taken into the human body would lead to serious alteration of sex characteristics and glands.

The animals are injected with antibiotics and tranquilizers. Antibiotics are commonly used in medicine to fight disease and infection. They are included in animal feed, especially for poultry and calves, to ward off any possible epidemic. While these drugs are important in treatment, indiscriminate intake of antibiotics into the system leads to strains of resistant bacteria, destruction of helpful bacteria, and possible allergic reactions to the drugs themselves. The flesh of animals injected with an antibiotic may contain these resistant bacteria in addition to the drug itself after their death.

The feed given to animals may contain residues of potentially deadly substances; among these are arsenic; chemical pesticides, including DDT; and mercury compounds. The consumption of animal fat is largely responsible for the high levels of DDT in the human body.

Very few animals are raised in a natural setting on naturally grown grain.

Canned and processed meats are further subjected to preservatives, chemical flavorings, and artificial enzymatic tenderizers. Nitrite coloring agents, illegal in fresh meat, are often added to these products.

For these reasons the menus here are vegetarian, or meatless. You can get an adequate supply of all nutrients without eating meat as these menus show; however, if you do choose to eat meat, seek out a place that sells organic meat—it is available in many health food stores.

Fish: Fish are not subjected to artificially created environments or treated, unnatural foods. This would seemingly make them ideal for consumption, but man has succeeded in contaminating the water making much of the haul unfit for human consumption. Deep-sea fish are the safest to eat. Eat only fresh fish; reject both frozen and canned, as the processing destroys natural enzymes and is likely to include chemicals.

Fruits and Vegetables: Buy organically grown produce whenever possible. This means fruits and vegetables grown in soil that is farmed without chemical fertilizers and crops that are not sprayed with pesticides, all indisputably poisonous to the human body. These pesticides are used because they are deadly to some forms of life, a good reason to suspect their effect on our bodies. In addition to the natural toxicity of these agricultural poisons, it is not known whether these chemicals, once taken into the plant or animal system and combined with other substances, produce a more toxic compound.

More and more health food stores are putting in organic produce. If there is no available outlet near you, contact sources that ship by mail. Many fruit and vegetable stores sell or have access to organically grown produce. Perhaps if you and your friends ask, the local store will accommodate your needs. If you live in a big city where there is little access to home-grown produce a nice trip for a day or weekend can be planned around a country shopping spree. Check in your area for farms which encourage visitors to come and pick their own fruits and vegetables. The fresh air and exercise alone will be good for you. These fruits and vegetables are the very freshest and are usually sold at lower prices than the local market selection. This is a good opportunity to stock up on tomatoes for sauce or soup which can be frozen for the winter, when fresh vine-ripened tomatoes are hard to find.

If you do buy fruits and vegetables which have been chemically treated (the supermarket and most fruit stand varieties), wash them well in *warm* water and, if necessary, peel them. This will help remove some surface contamination. Those pesticides taken in through the roots, of course, will remain.

Flour: Don't buy white flour and products which are dependent on the use of white flour. Wheat was once a staple of this country. Today, the most nourishing part of the wheat—most of the protein, the fat, the B and E vitamins and the iron and phosphorus found in the wheat germ and bran coating is removed when creating white flour. The remaining endosperm is composed mainly of carbohydrate and protein. To understand the significance of this a bit of detail is necessary. Proteins are complex nitrogen containing substances made of amino acids. There are two forms of protein, complete—containing all the amino acids considered essential for life which cannot be produced by the body itself, and incomplete—those lacking one or more essential amino acid. There are two proteins found in wheat—gliadin, an incomplete protein, and glutenin, a complete protein. Glutenin is particularly concentrated in the bran and germ. The protein value of the whole grain is, therefore of higher quality. The bran, in addition, serves as a natural laxative.

In producing white flour, after the health-giving elements are removed in milling, the flour is treated with a chemical bleaching agent to obtain pure white flour. This bleaching destroys any remaining vitamin content and acts to sterilize the flour so insects will not grow in it. They will not grow because all of the life-supporting elements have been removed. What is left is a substance that, when baked, forms a product which we have been taught to call "white bread"; while it certainly is white, the only similarity between it and bread is purely coincidental.

Enriched flour has some of the destroyed nutrients restored—the iron, thiamin, riboflavin, and niacin. With the exception of riboflavin the levels are still considerably lower than those in the original wheat.

Choose instead whole wheat flour, potato starch or flour, corn flour, unbolted corn meal, and, if you like, buckwheat and soy flour. There are specialty uses for rice and chestnut flours but these needn't be considered kitchen staples. Stone-ground flours undergo the least amount of vitamin and mineral loss during milling. To prevent spoilage or rancidity store whole grain flour in a cool, dry place or refrigerator if it is to be kept for any length of time.

Sweeteners: Do not use refined white sugar. White sugar consists of pure carbohydrate without any vitamins, minerals, or other elements that make food good for you. The sugar cane is so highly refined that all the minerals and vitamins are extracted and all that remains is a sweet taste and calories. Obesity, tooth decay, and diabetes are among the many diseases related to large consumption of refined sugar. In the digestive system refined white sugar, robbed of the natural vitamin B and calcium of the cane, comes to the cells as concentrated pure sugar, providing no nourishment and possibly contributing to cell starvation.

Sweeten your food instead with honey, unsulphured molasses (West Indies or Barbados varieties are milder, more mellow than blackstrap), pure maple syrup, and "raw, unrefined" sugar. The health benefits of the commonly available raw sugar are widely disputed. Pure unrefined sugar cannot be marketed in this country. The sugar sold as "raw" or "unrefined" is actually partially refined with some of the molasses added back. It is just a trace better than white sugar and should be used sparingly or only when no other sweetener will do.

Strained, or uncooked, honey (indicated as such on the label) refers to the manufacturing process. Strained honey is not subjected to heat so the native pollen grains and enzymes are not destroyed. Don't be dismayed if crystals begin to form in the jar—they only indicate that the honey hasn't been processed. To dissolve crystals place the jar of honey in warm water for a few minutes. Honey is available in a variety of flavors depending upon the flowers the bees gathered the nectar from. Clover and tupelo are the mildest. Experiment with a few varieties to find your favorite.

For sweet spreads try fruit butters and pure preserves, jams and jellies made with whole fruits, natural juices, honey, and lemon juice. They are free from preservatives and artificial coloring. These can be found at health food outlets and are delicious.

Baked Goods: Whenever possible bake your own breads, cookies, and cakes with whole grains and natural sweeteners. You can enrich these items by adding rolled oats and wheat germ. Non-aluminum baking powder (a leavening agent made without added aluminum salts) and yeast with no preservatives can be purchased at health food stores. Many people prefer not to use baking powder or soda since the change it causes in the acidity during baking reduces the thiamin content of the product. However the baked goods made with these leavening agents have a softer texture and some people find them more easily digestible. The choice is an individual one.

The United States government has set certain standards, a basic formula, for commercial breads. As a result the label need not list many chemicals and artificial ingredients which are included. Preservatives, or fresheners, coloring and flavoring agents, however, must be listed. If they are, don't buy the bread. Many brands do offer a list of ingredients. If they don't they most likely have nothing to boast about. Even if they do, be wary—it need not be a complete list.

Buy whole grain breads made with honey and molasses as sweeteners. There are some commercially packaged breads which meet these standards. Most neighborhood stores stock 100 percent whole wheat bread and others described as "Old World" or "Country Style" rye or pumpernickel which state on the label "no preservatives added." Bread made with clean, wholesome ingredients does not need preservatives. Many hard-crust Italian and Vienna loaves are made with unbleached flour and no sugar or shortening. This may be stated on the label. They are often called "Home Loaves." Fresh bakery breads do not use preservatives but some bakers do add coloring agents and dough conditioners. Ask at your local bakery—most bakers are eager to talk about their art. Health food stores offer dozens of interesting breads which you'll enjoy trying.

Stone-ground whole grain crackers are widespread in the supermarket. The imported varieties are especially good, often called Norwegian or Scandinavian flat breads or crisps.

Unlike bread, there are no government standards for cakes and cookies so chemicals can be added at will. These products must list all ingredients, however, so you can see for yourself what you are getting. Delicious, wholesome alternatives are available in your health food store.

Processed Foods: Food manufacturing has become big business today, made possible only by the use of additives. The additives prevent aging, make use of machinery easier (as dough conditioners), reduce time and costs, restore properties destroyed by elaborate processing, and disguise those that cannot be restored. Some additives are added to make the use of other additives possible! An additive can change taste and texture to the point that totally synthetic foods can and have been created. Therefore, in selecting food you must not only be concerned with what is missing, but with what is added as well. In general, bypass processed foods when you buy groceries. Foods that are processed have been treated or prepared in some way.

Read the ingredients on the labels of all foods. Reject those which contain white flour; refined sugar; corn syrup; fresheners and preservatives such as calcium propionate, BHT, BHA, sodium benzoate, benzoic acid; mono- and di-glycerides or other emulsifiers, prevalent in imitation dairy products; gum tragacanth and other gums; aluminum-based baking powders; artificial color or flavor; flavor enhancers such as MSG, hydrolized vegetable protein, and disodium inosinates and glyanates. Unfortunately many chemicals are permitted that need not be mentioned on the label. Irradiation, another method of preservation, exposes food to ionizing rays possibly linked to cancer. It's easy to kid yourself that the small amount of chemical added to the food is harmless. Each chemical, however, has a specific job to do so many products have several different substances added. These are then combined with a number of other artificially treated products, each with several additives, to make a recipe and a combination of these dishes makes a meal . . . day after day. The infinitesimal amount of chemical additive mushrooms into a frightening ingestion of unnatural substances. No scientist will deny that large doses of these additives are poisonous. A small amount retained by the system eventually becomes a large dose. Although immediate and observable symptoms may not be exhibited, there is a strong likelihood that subtle cell changes are taking place. Any toxic substance places a burden on the organs, causing unwarranted wear and tear. The body's ability to deal with these substances varies with the individual. Some systems can withstand abuse; some can't. WARNING: EATING MAY BE HARMFUL TO YOUR HEALTH.

The packaging itself is another factor in food selection. In addition to the detrimental effects packaging has had on the environment, it contributes to the presence of unintentional food additives. These come from fillers in paper and cardboard, glues, adhesives, and plasticizers. Government regulation of food additives and packaging is far from satisfactory.

Besides these things that have been deliberately added, heat, pressure, peeling, shredding, and other processes employed in the packaging tend to destroy much of the vitamin and mineral content. Buy fresh fruit and vegetables instead of canned or frozen and, although neither is recommended, frozen over canned. Canned varieties exhibit greater loss of vitamin C and thiamin and rely on the addition of calcium salts to improve texture. Both processes damage enzymes in the food.

Avoid confectionary products, soft drinks, and candy on your grocer's shelf. These foods are doctored with chemicals and rely heavily on white flour and sugar. They contribute least to a good nutritional plan. Avoid precooked convenience foods—instant foods, frozen dinners, and cake mixes. They are loaded with chemicals.

Cereals: Like wheat, all cereal grains are seeds composed of an inner portion, or endosperm, a germ, and a protective seed coat known as the bran. Choose whole grain cereals and grains that are free from preservatives. Both Wheatena and Old Fashioned Quaker Oats meet these requirements. Commercial dry cereals are mostly air and starch. The protein has deteriorated because of excessive heat, flaking, and puffing, not to mention the totally unnecessary preservatives, emulsifiers, and sweeteners that are added. For cold cereals try the Swiss breakfast cereals or make your own by combining toasted oats, wheat germ, chopped almonds, shredded coconut, and raisins or dried fruits. A particularly popular blend of raw cereal grains is called Crunchy Granola and is available at all health food outlets. You'll never go back to cornflakes!

Grains and pasta products are important foods used alone, with vegetables or cheese, and in soups. Buckwheat groats (kasha), cracked wheat (bulghur), and brown (unhulled) rice are available in most markets. For varieties grown in fields free from chemicals visit your health food source. Whole wheat and soy noodles and macaroni products made with an artichoke pulp base are also available in health food stores and taste just like the ones you're used to. Also, whole (unhulled, not pearled) barley and millet add variety to the diet.

Dairy Products: Use the freshest dairy products you can get—milk, butter, cream, and eggs right from the farm are the healthiest. Supermarket eggs are rarely fresh and bare no flavor resemblance to those just in from the poultry farm. Chickens confined and fed scientifically produce eggs with pale yolks causing chicken farmers to add synthetic dyes to the feed for richer color. Fertile eggs from organically raised chickens are worth the extra pennies. They are alive and therefore contain life-sustaining enzymes not present in unfertile eggs.

Raw (unpasteurized) certified milk is sold in health food stores. Many people feel this milk is the most nutritious since the heat used in pasteurization destroys some vitamin content, notably vitamin C and thiamin. It is interesting to note that pasteurized milk will spoil naturally before it sours (a change caused by nonharmful acid-forming bacteria) while its raw counterpart sours before it spoils. Spoiled milk is useless. Sour milk can be used for baking and making cottage cheese. The word "Certified" indicates the milk is clean—free from dirt and from harmful bacteria. If you're using the milk for cooking there is no point in buying raw milk. Dry milk powder is useful in cooking and baking. Products made from goat's milk are less contaminated than those from cow's milk, due to the methods of animal raising.

Natural cheese is cheese made directly from milk. The best of these are Parmesan, Cheddar, curd and cream cheese, goat cheese, and the many imported varieties. Health food stores offer organic cheeses made from raw milk. Many are salt free and some tend to be rather bland. Processed cheese and cheese spreads are made by blending and heating one or more varieties of natural cheese with additives, including emulsifiers, artificial coloring, and preservatives. Other food elements may also be added.

Although butter is high in saturated fat, often linked to heart disease, it is a naturally saturated fat and preferable to margarine.

Margarine is made from vegetable oil which is hydrogenated to obtain a solid fat. The process of hydrogenation brings about saturation, although not complete saturation. In addition, margarine is treated with preservatives; mono- and di-glycerides or lecithin, which are chemically made fats added as emulsifiers; butter flavor; and artificial coloring.

Yoghurt is another healthy, versatile product to keep in mind. Its nutritional value is equal to that of the milk from which it is made and can be enhanced by the addition of dry milk powder when made at home. It is said by many to have excellent medicinal qualities, keeps the intestinal system healthy and is used in great quantities in the Balkans and Near East where the people attribute their heartiness and longevity to this constant consumption of yoghurt. Plain yoghurt is the only kind to buy and is available in all food stores. Freshly made, the flavor is much richer and such yoghurt is worth seeking out. Often delicacy stores and Mideast groceries offer the best varieties. It's ideal for salads with vegetables, in soups, or as a dessert with honey and wheat germ to taste.

Seasoning: Try growing your own herbs in a window box, and your own bean sprouts. Sprouts are high in nutrition and low in calories—great in salads, soups, vegetable combinations and as snacks. Buy fresh herbs whenever you can. Use fresh garlic, fresh onion, and fresh lemon juice. Buy dried herbs in small quantity—their goodness is short lived. For longest life store them in tightly covered jars away from heat. Season with sun-ripened sea salt which contains all the native minerals. Common table salt is bleached and may contain a chemical to prevent caking. Kosher salt is coarse-grained sea salt with natural iodine and minerals. It can be used instead of sea salt in cooking, and when sprinkled on foods the coarse grain creates an attractive sparkle. If you prefer Kosher salt to fine-grained sea salt use a little less at first as the flavor is more pronounced, and adjust later if necessary. The desire for salt is acquired and if need be the palate can become accustomed to less. If you wish to reduce salt intake try using more herbs. Synthetic salts and flavoring agents will be unnecessary. Veg-Sal and Spike, both available in health food stores, provide a combination of herbs and spices excellent for perking up eggs, dips, soups, and vegetable combinations.

Vegetable bouillon cubes can be used for additional flavoring in cooking if you like, but watch the label here for chemical additives and artificial flavorings. Acceptable varieties are available in health food stores.

Use Tamari or pure soy sauce, which has only water, whole wheat flour, and salt added.

Salad Dressing: Make your own salad dressing and sauces. Manufactured varieties contain sugar, thickening agents, vegetable gums, and a sequestrant known as EDTA, which has been traced as a cause of calcium inbalance and kidney disorders.

Select 100 percent pure unsaturated vegetable oils which are unrefined. Refined oils are treated with alkali and bleached. The best quality oil is from the first (cold) pressing. Cheaper oils are extracted by chemicals or steam. Safflower, corn, soy, sesame seed, and peanut oil are the highest in unsaturates. Olive oil is fine for salads and cooking where specified; unlike other oils it does have a characteristic flavor. Although cottonseed oil is unsaturated it is a poor choice for human consumption. Cotton, not thought of as a food crop, is doused with chemical sprays. Varieties called "vegetable oil" contain a high percentage of cottonseed oil. Solid vegetable shortenings are hydrogenated (partially saturated) and are laced with chemicals.

Small amounts of pure cider, malt, and wine vinegar are harmless. If you prefer, lemon or lime juice are fine substitutes.

Beverages: Squeeze your own juices or buy pure juices with no sweeteners or preservatives. Besides making the traditional citrus juices a juice extractor, which can be purchased for $50 to $150, can turn any fruit or vegetable (or combination of them) into juice.

Health food stores offer a variety of untreated vegetable and fruit juices but these are expensive. Look for pure apple cider; also, Red Cheek Apple Juice, available in many markets. A blender is very useful for homemade juices, a juice extractor a beautiful luxury. Fruit drinks on the grocer's shelf sport such names as nectars, ades, juice-drinks, juice cocktail, ad infinitum. They are mostly water with a small percent of real fruit juice. Flavor enhancers help them taste like juice and many contain artificial color, preservatives, and citric acid and sugar which are bad for your teeth.

Decaffeinated coffee or cereal beverages can replace regular coffee. Cereal beverage is a soluble extract made from ground grains and tastes surprisingly like coffee. It is quite good and satisfies the coffee craving.

Loose tea or tea that is sold in bags at health food outlets or specialty stores is preferable. Many American packaged teas contain as much caffeine as coffee. This is not true of herb teas. In addition, dyes used in tea bags contain cancer-linked substances which though minuscule in quantity are obviously potentially harmful to the human system. Individual tea strainers are sold everywhere and are just as easy to use as tea bags.

Dried Fruits and Nuts: For snacking serve nuts, seeds, and unsulphured dried fruits as well as fresh fruits. Nuts are most healthful eaten unroasted, unsalted, and unoiled. Health food outlets and some imported specialty shops offer organically grown varieties. Place raw nuts, seeds, and fruits in bowls around the room for friends to help themselves.

Nut butters should have no additives and should be made with unhydrogenated oil. If you have a blender they are easy to make at home. Just process nuts at high speed adding a little oil until desired consistency is reached. You'll be delighted by the fresh, nutty flavor, not at all artificially sweet like the commercial varieties. The oil may separate out of pure nut butter since no chemical emulsifier has been added. Just stir it in before spreading.

Candy: For those who can't resist sweets, a variety of nutritious candies are sold which are made with dried fruits, nuts, coconut, peanut butter, and carob (a chocolate substitute). There are also hard candies made with honey, raw sugar, lemon, and natural fruit flavors, free from corn syrup and artificial color found in their concentrated sugar counterparts. All are available at health food outlets. Keep these sweets at a minimum though.

Halvah, a Mideastern confection made with sesame seed paste, is another excellent choice.

WHEN YOU EAT OUT

Most of us do not eat all our meals at home. Eating out limits some of the control you have over your food choices, but there is no reason you can't carry the vegetarian-health patterns you have established into the world outside your kitchen.

If a health food or dairy restaurant is convenient this will naturally be your first choice.

Cafeterias provide a wide selection of dishes, particularly salads and hot vegetable entrees to choose from. Many of the vegetables in season are fresh. Inquire.

When eating in a coffee shop there is usually a selection of eggs, tossed salads with oil and vinegar, cottage cheese with fresh fruit or vegetables, and a variety of cheese sandwiches on whole wheat bread. If you've never had grilled Swiss cheese on whole wheat bread you have a treat in store! For variety, add tomato. Potato dishes are often on the menu. Baked potato with a side order of cottage cheese gives you a substantial lunch. Whole wheat toast, bran and corn muffins can round out the menu.

Foreign restaurants are a good choice, especially if you entertain others at mealtime. Mideastern restaurants have a number of healthy, meatless dishes to choose from; cheese stuffed pasta and salads make Italian restaurants a good possibility; Mexican staples include beans and rice, filled corn meal tortillas and avocado salads. Many Chinese restaurants serve combination vegetable, rice and vegetable, and noodle and vegetable dishes which have no meat. Be aware, however, Chinese cuisine often contains heavy doses of MSG. You may choose to eat fresh fish occasionally and this broadens your range when dining out. If you are ever in doubt about a dish ask. You'll find most waiters and waitresses fascinated and very helpful.

For a quick snack look for places that feature fresh-squeezed orange juice, kasha and potato knishes (a Jewish delicatessen specialty), Greek cheese, and spinach pies. Fallafel stands, common in the New York area, offer fried chick pea fritters and salad stuffed into Mideastern pita bread pockets and topped with tahini, a sesame seed sauce. This is a Mideastern specialty worth seeking out. In the South and West, taco stands offer cheese enchiladas, cheese stuffed corn meal tortillas with a hot Mexican sauce.

When you're invited to dinner be sure to tell whoever is responsible for the meal if you are a vegetarian. If they are bewildered and at a loss, it's easy enough to give some suggestions or, better still, a copy of this book. Most of the items on any menu are vegetarian to begin with—vegetables, salad, bread. You can remind them of the many elegant dishes that can be made with eggs and cheese. One of the exciting things about this way of eating is that it forces you (and your hosts) into trying new foods and breaking away from conventional eating habits. In any case, don't expect a perfect turnout, but you can be sure you'll fare better than if you are served a steak dinner.

II

Cooking with Natural Food

THE MENU

Here are a month's worth of meatless menus, complete with recipes and cooking hints, designed to make natural healthy eating easy. A series of interesting dishes have been put together to create thirty well-balanced, pleasing meals. These are menus and recipes that I developed originally for my own kitchen.

Each item on the menu is important for its contribution to the meal. If you choose not to prepare one of the dishes replace it with another similar in kind. For example, store-bought whole grain breads can be served instead of homemade or one variety of cheese can replace another. For other substitutions check the section AN ADEQUATE DIET which lists foods by the nutritional contribution they make to the diet.

The order in which the menus are presented will provide maximum variety from day to day. It will enable you to prepare certain foods in advance and use leftovers in future meals. From a nutritional standpoint, however, the order can be changed or any menu repeated at will.

If at any time you find you would like larger meals than are suggested here melon, fresh fruit sections or a small cup of soup can be served first. Whole grain breads can be added where they are not specifically mentioned. Fruit and vegetable juices, water, and tea can be served at any meal. Where a beverage goes especially well with the meal it is suggested in the menu.

There are no desserts included in these menus since a meal should be nutritionally complete without dessert. This does not mean that desserts are forbidden. Fruits and fruit dishes, cakes and cookies made with whole grains and unrefined sweeteners, dried fruits and nuts, whole grain breads with sweet spreads, and homemade puddings are all perfectly acceptable foods; and, as a matter of fact, they are good for you. A special chapter of additional homemade desserts follows the menu section.

By following the menus and guidelines which begin on the next page, calories and food values will look after themselves and you can devote your energies to trying out the new ideas and eventually adding some of your own.

N.B. Before you begin these menus read over section III, Natural Food Expertise. There you will find important cooking advice designed to make you an expert in the kitchen.

Menu #1

GINGERED MELON
COUNTRY POTATO PIE
SALAD WITH VINAIGRETTE DRESSING
WHOLE WHEAT ROLLS

Serving Suggestions: This dinner for four is perfect for company as well as family dinner.

Cooking Schedule: Rolls can be made well in advance and frozen successfully. Remove them from freezer ½ hour before dinner and warm in oven 5 minutes before serving. When baking rolls for use the same day, begin at least 3 hours before they are to be served.

Begin Potato Pie 1 hour before dinner; preparation time is 15 to 20 minutes. To prepare early in the day follow special instructions given and allow 5 to 10 minutes to assemble before 45-minute baking period.

Dressing takes 5 minutes to prepare and can be made just before needed or early in the day and refrigerated.

Prepare salad and melon while pie bakes.

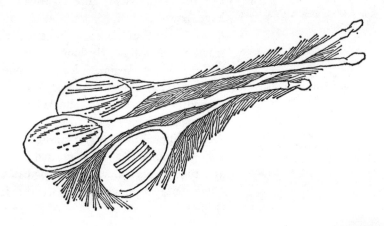

You've decided to make homemade rolls! Try these—they will dispel any fears you have about breadmaking because no matter what, you'll find they're always delicious.

WHOLE WHEAT ROLLS

Utensils: large baking sheet or muffin tin
Yield: 24 rolls or 12 rolls and 1 braided bread
Preparation time: 30 minutes
Rising time: 1 hour and 45 minutes
Baking time: 15 minutes
Oven temperature: 400° F.

1¼ cups milk
¼ cup raw sugar
2½ teaspoons salt
3 tablespoons honey
¼ cup butter
½ cup water

2 tablespoons (2 packages) dry yeast
Approximately 4 cups whole wheat flour
Melted butter
Sesame seeds

[1] For a work surface that's easy to clean and guaranteed to prevent bread and pastry dough from sticking, cover work area with a piece of oilcloth.

[2] To knead dough: rub a little flour on hands, then form dough into a ball. Flatten. Fold dough toward you. Using heels of hands, push dough away with a rolling motion and fold over itself. Give the dough a quarter turn. Repeat the process for about 10 minutes, until dough is elastic and springs back when pressed lightly with fingers. If dough be-

Heat together milk, sugar, salt, honey, butter and water until tiny bubbles begin to form around edge. Cool slightly. In a large bowl, mix the yeast and 2 cups flour. Add the milk mixture and stir until smooth. Stir in enough flour to make a stiff dough that begins to leave the sides of the bowl as you stir. Turn on to a well floured board or oilcloth[1] and knead until dough no longer sticks to your hands.[2] Add additional flour as you knead to prevent sticking.[3] Place in greased bowl and turn so that all surfaces are greased. Cover with clean cloth and let rise in warm place until doubled, about 45 minutes. The inside of an unlit oven is the perfect place. Push dough down and shape into rolls.[4] Brush tops with melted butter, cover with towel and let rise again 1 hour. Sprinkle sesame seeds on top. Bake rolls in 400° F. oven 15 minutes, braid 45. Remove from pan and cool on wire rack.

comes too sticky to manage, sprinkle more flour on hands and board.

[3] The amount of flour needed varies each time with the flour itself and is determined by feel. Use just enough to form a dough that can be kneaded without sticking. Add more if necessary as you knead.

[4] To shape rolls: *Cloverleaf:* form dough into round balls the size of walnuts. Place 3 balls in each greased muffin cup.
Parker House: Roll dough ¼-inch thick. Cut in 3-inch rounds. Make a light cut in dough with back of knife slightly off center. Fold so smaller half overlaps larger, lower half. Press tightly at ends of crease to prevent spreading. Place close together on greased baking sheet.
Dinner: Form dough into cylindrical shapes with tapered ends. Place 1 inch apart on lightly greased baking sheet.
Braid: Use half of dough to make a braid. Divide into thirds and roll between palms to form 3 ropes. Pinch ropes together at one end. Weave lengths together as you would plait hair. Pinch ends together at end of braid. Place on lightly greased baking sheet in a half circle like a horseshoe.

Country Potato Pie is a cross between potato pudding and a quiche. The result, a delicate cheesy custard on a flavorful potato base.

COUNTRY POTATO PIE

Utensils: blender or coarse grater; 9-inch pie plate
Yield: 4 servings
Preparation time: 15 to 20 minutes
Baking time: 40 to 45 minutes
Oven temperature: 375° F.

2 *tablespoons butter*	1 *cup milk*
3 *medium potatoes, peeled*	½ *teaspoon pepper*
1½ *teaspoons salt*	2 *tablespoons chopped*
1 *cup (¼ pound) shredded*	*parsley*
Swiss cheese	½ *teaspoon paprika*
½ *cup chopped onion*	½ *teaspoon dry mustard*
2 *eggs*	

To prepare in advance: Place shredded potatoes in bowl with cold water to cover and refrigerate to prevent darkening. Drain well before using. Reserve cooked onion in covered pan. Beat eggs, milk and seasonings and keep in refrigerator. Assemble 5 to 10 minutes before baking.

[5] To grate potatoes in blender see directions for potato pancakes (see Index).

[6] Do not serve the Potato Pie before it has a chance to cool slightly. The taste is

Spread 1 tablespoon butter over bottom and side of 9-inch pie plate. Shred potatoes in blender or on coarse grater;[5] drain well. Sprinkle 1 teaspoon salt on potatoes. Press over bottom and side of pie plate to form crust. Sprinkle cheese over potato crust. Melt remaining 1 tablespoon butter in skillet. Add onion and cook until tender and transparent. Spread over cheese. Beat eggs with remaining ½ teaspoon salt, milk, pepper, parsley, paprika, and mustard. Pour over onion and cheese in pie plate. Bake in 375° F. oven

40 to 45 minutes until edge of pie is golden and knife inserted in center comes out clean. Let stand 10 minutes before serving.[6] masked when hot and must be allowed to cool slightly for terrific results.

SALAD WITH VINAIGRETTE DRESSING

Prepare salad for 4 using 1 small head lettuce, diced tomatoes, sliced cucumber, and green pepper strips. Add the following dressing at serving time.

1 cup oil
½ cup wine vinegar
2 tablespoons lemon juice

¼ teaspoon pepper
½ cup chopped parsley

Combine all ingredients and shake well. Shake again before pouring.

GINGERED MELON

Cut pieces of honeydew melon to desired size. Fruit is most flavorful at room temperature so take melon out of refrigerator at least 15 minutes before dinner to remove chill. Sprinkle each piece with ¼ teaspoon ground ginger. Serve with lemon wedges. Serve melon when pie is removed from oven.

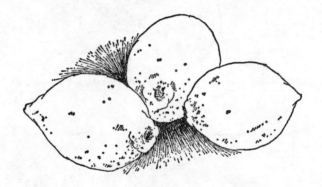

Menu #2

YOGHURT SOUP
VEGETABLE COUSCOUS
PITA AND KASHCAVEL

Serving Suggestions: This food borrows from the Algerian and Arab cuisines. Serve the soup while the other dishes finish cooking. Cooked couscous and vegetable sauce can be kept in a covered pot, removed from heat, for several minutes until serving, if need be.

Cooking Schedule: Unflavored yoghurt is available all over, but just in case you'd like to try making your own, directions are given. It should be made the day before you want to use it and can be stored about 5 days.

The soup is made first, at least 1 hour before dinner or earlier in the day. Although it can be made up to 15 minutes before, the flavor develops as it stands and it will not be as tasty.

Start soaking the couscous grain about 50 minutes prior to dinner. You needn't begin actual preparation, however, until 30 minutes before you'll be ready to serve the main course.

The Pita and Kashcavel can be made at the last minute and warmed while you enjoy the soup.

Homemade yoghurt is more delicate and more nutritious than the commercial kind and a snap to make. Any plain yoghurt can serve as a starter.

HOMEMADE YOGHURT

Utensils: deep casserole
Yield: 1 quart
Preparation time: 15 minutes
Waiting time: 4½ hours[1]

1 quart milk, regular, skim or reconstituted dry
½ cup non-fat dry milk powder
¼ cup plain yoghurt[2]

Combine milk and dry milk powder in small saucepan, bring to boil, remove from heat and cool to lukewarm, about 15 minutes. Add small amount of lukewarm milk to plain yoghurt starter and beat lightly with fork or wire whip. Add to remaining cooled milk and beat briefly. Pour into a deep casserole, cover with a clean cloth and secure cloth over casserole with a rubber band. Place in unlit oven for 4½ hours for culture to grow. After yoghurt has fermented place in refrigerator to chill before using.

[1] The longer you let the yoghurt ferment the more tart it becomes: 4½ hours gives a mild product; for more tartness increase fermenting time to taste. The more culture you use the quicker the action.

[2] Any yoghurt can be used as a starter. Save a small amount of the homemade to start the next batch.

The soup is cold with a distinctive cucumber taste and aroma. The chopped nuts add interesting texture. A nice main dish for a luncheon as well as first course for dinner.

YOGHURT SOUP

Yield: 4 servings
Preparation time: 5 minutes

2 *cups plain yoghurt*
¼ *cup coarsely chopped*
   walnuts
1 *cup peeled, diced*
   cucumber[3]

1 *clove garlic, crushed*
½ *teaspoon salt*

Beat yoghurt with a wire whip or fork until smooth. Stir in remaining ingredients and chill. Place 1 ice cube in each plate with soup to serve.

[3] When dicing cucumber remove as many seeds as possible as they may add a bitter taste.

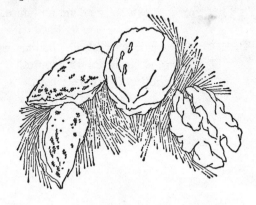

Couscous is a fine cereal grain which resembles farina in texture. It is a staple of North Africa, quite bland in itself, but excellent when topped with this aromatic vegetable melange. The raisins add the finishing touch.

COUSCOUS

Utensils: large saucepan; colander; cheesecloth
Yield: 4 servings
Soaking time: 20 minutes
Cooking time: 30 minutes

1 cup couscous[4]
1 cup water
1 teaspoon salt

2 tablespoons butter
Vegetable Sauce (recipe
    follows)

[4] Fine semolina can be used instead of couscous.

[5] Vegetable broth can be used to steam couscous instead of water for added flavor.

[6] If you prefer, prepare couscous according to package directions.

Place couscous in bowl and stir in water and salt. Soak until water is absorbed, about 20 minutes. Rub grain between fingers so there are no lumps. Place couscous in a colander lined with cheesecloth, place over slowly boiling water,[5] cover and steam for 30 minutes.[6] To serve, add butter to cooked couscous, mound on plates and top with Vegetable Sauce.

VEGETABLE SAUCE

Preparation time: 10 minutes[7]
Cooking time: 30 minutes

2 tablespoons butter[8]
1 onion, chopped
2 tomatoes, cubed
1 green pepper, diced
2 carrots, peeled if necessary
   and sliced crosswise

1 zucchini, cubed
1 teaspoon salt
¼ teaspoon pepper or pepper
   sauce
8 mushrooms
¼ cup raisins

Heat butter in saucepan. Add onion and cook until tender. Add tomatoes, green pepper, carrots, zucchini, salt, and pepper. Cover and cook over low heat 15 minutes. Add mushrooms and raisins, cover and cook until all vegetables are tender, 5 to 10 minutes.

[7] Prepare vegetables in order given, so that as onions cook the others can be readied.

[8] Butter is preferable in the recipe for flavor, however, if you prefer oil can be used.

Pita is a flat Syrian bread available in Mideastern groceries, most delicatessens, and many supermarkets. When cut in half crosswise it can be opened to form a pocket. The Kashcavel is a hard white cheese popular in Turkey, Rumania and the Balkan countries which adds new dimension to your cheese repertoire. If Kashcavel is unavailable substitute any hard white cheese or a mild Cheddar.

PITA AND KASHCAVEL

Slice pita crosswise and open pocket. Insert pieces of cheese to fill pocket. Place in 300° F. oven until cheese melts, about 5 minutes. Serve hot, allowing ½ small bread per person.

Menu #3

MUSHROOM CUTLETS WITH SOUR CREAM SAUCE
PAN-FRIED ASPARAGUS
PICKLED BEETS

Cooking Schedule: Pickled Beets should be chilled at least 1 hour before serving, and can be kept under refrigeration about 2 weeks. The beets themselves take 30 to 40 minutes to cook. Consequently this dish should be prepared from 2 hours to 2 weeks before needed.

Begin Mushroom Cutlets 45 minutes before dinner. While they are baking the sauce and asparagus can be made.

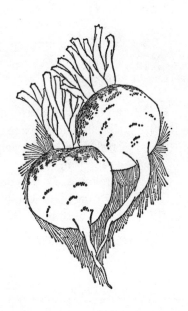

Pickled Beets provide a pungent side dish, especially appealing when sour cream dishes appear on the menu. They call for very little actual work and keep well for a handy meal accompaniment alone or on top of a green salad.

PICKLED BEETS

Yield: 4 servings
Preparation time: under 10 minutes
Cooking time: 30 to 40 minutes

2 large fresh beets (about 1 pound)
1 small onion, thinly sliced
¼ cup cider vinegar
¼ cup water or beet liquid
1 tablespoon honey or raw sugar
½ teaspoon salt
4 cloves
½ bay leaf

[1] Peeled beets bleed (lose their color) when cooked and should be left whole, unpeeled unless the liquid is to be used.

[2] Peel will easily slip off cooked beets.

Scrub beets and trim root and stem ends without cutting into the bulb.[1] Place in saucepan with water to cover. Bring to boil, cover and cook 30 to 40 minutes, until tender. Peel[2] and slice. Cut each slice in half. Place in shallow casserole or bowl. Combine remaining ingredients in a saucepan, bring to boil, cover and cook 5 minutes. Pour cooked onions and liquid over beets. Chill 1 hour before serving. To store, keep chilled mixture in covered jar in refrigerator.

Two Mushroom Cutlets provide a very substantial meat substitute. Extras can be frozen up to 3 months, but they're most flavorful fresh. Top with Sour Cream Sauce.

MUSHROOM CUTLETS

Utensils: blender; baking sheet
Yield: 8 cutlets; 4 servings
Preparation time: 20 minutes
Baking time: 20 minutes
Oven temperature: 350° F.

1 large or 2 small potatoes
(1 cup diced)
2 medium onions, chopped
2 tablespoons butter
1 pound mushrooms,
chopped
2 eggs
¼ cup wheat germ

1 cup whole wheat bread
crumbs[3]
1 teaspoon salt
¼ teaspoon pepper
½ teaspoon dried leaf thyme
2 tablespoons chopped
parsley

[3] Make 1 cup whole wheat bread crumbs by grating 3 slices stale whole wheat bread on grater or in blender.

[4] Reserve remaining ½ cup onion-mushroom mixture for sauce.

Place unpeeled, quartered potatoes in saucepan in salted water to cover. Bring to boil, reduce heat and cook, uncovered, until tender, but not mushy, 15 to 20 minutes. Meanwhile, sauté onion in 1 tablespoon butter in skillet until tender. Add mushrooms, remaining tablespoon butter, cover, and cook over low heat 10 to 15 minutes, until tender. Reserve 1 cup of the mixture, draining liquid back into the pan. Peel cooked potato and dice. Place potato, remaining onion-mushroom mixture with liquid, and eggs in blender container and blend at high speed until smooth. Turn into bowl and add wheat germ, bread crumbs, seasonings, and ½ cup reserved mushroom mixture.[4] Mix thoroughly. Place mixture in 8 mounds, ⅓ cup each, on greased baking sheet. Bake in 350° F. oven 20 minutes. Serve hot with Sour Cream Sauce.

SOUR CREAM SAUCE

Preparation and cooking time: 5 minutes

1 cup sour cream
½ cup reserved onion-
   mushroom mixture

1 tablespoon lemon juice
½ teaspoon salt
¼ teaspoon pepper

Combine all ingredients in small saucepan. Heat gently until warmed through. Do not boil.

PAN-FRIED ASPARAGUS

For four servings, trim 1½ to 2 pounds asparagus and slice into 1½-inch lengths. Melt 2 tablespoons butter in skillet and sauté asparagus over high heat until crisp-tender, about 5 minutes. Stir frequently. Season well with salt and lots of freshly ground pepper.

Menu #4

ITALIAN SPINACH OMELET
CORN ON THE COB
WHOLE WHEAT ITALIAN BREAD

Serving Suggestions: An elegant meal with no fuss and very little time involved; ideal for family or unexpected guests.

Cooking Schedule: A little chopping, slicing and grating of cheese is the only work involved. So, start 25 minutes before you want to eat, allowing about 10 minutes for the work and 15 minutes to cook.

Put up a big pot of water to boil when you begin. The corn can be cooked while the eggs set.

An omelet, transformed into a gourmet's delight. This *frittata* as the Italians call it, is delicate, but very satisfying. What's more, it looks beautiful.

ITALIAN SPINACH OMELET

Utensils: large skillet and spatula
Yield: 4 servings
Preparation time: under 10 minutes
Cooking time: 15 minutes

3 tablespoons olive oil
¾ cup thinly sliced small white onions
8 eggs
1½ cups coarsely chopped raw spinach
½ teaspoon salt
¼ teaspoon pepper
¼ teaspoon dried basil

2 tablespoons chopped parsley
⅓ cup freshly grated Parmesan cheese
2 firm tomatoes, thinly sliced
8 black olives, pitted and thinly sliced

Heat oil in heavy skillet. Cook onion over medium heat until transparent. Beat eggs with a wire whip and fold in spinach, salt, pepper, basil, parsley, and cheese. Pour into skillet and cook over low heat, gently lifting edges as egg sets, allowing soft egg to run down, until partially set, about 3 minutes. Arrange tomato slices and olives on top in circular fashion. Place under broiler, about 3 inches from heat, until set and lightly browned on top, about 5 minutes. Cut into wedges and serve directly from skillet.[1]

[1] Leftovers can be chilled, cut into small wedges and served as hors d'oeuvre or appetizer.

CORN ON THE COB

[2] Salt tends to harden kernels so do not add to cooking water.

Bring a large pot of unsalted water[2] to rapid boil. Allow 1 ear of corn per person. Remove husks and silks from corn just before cooking. Clean under cold water to make shucking easier. If desired add husks from one ear to pot for added flavor. Place corn in boiling water. Cook at gentle boil until kernels are tender, about 5 minutes. Drain and serve immediately with plenty of butter, salt and paprika for freshest flavor.

WHOLE WHEAT ITALIAN BREAD

Fresh baked whole wheat Italian bread is available in many Italian bakeries, groceries, and recently in health food stores. If desired warm in moderate (300° F.) oven about 3 minutes, until crisp and heated through. If unavailable substitute whole wheat crackers or bread sticks.

Menu #5

FRIED BROWN RICE AND VEGETABLES
CABBAGE SALAD WITH CARROT DRESSING
JAPANESE TEA

Serving Suggestions: This is an excellent way to use up odds and ends of vegetables that have accumulated.

For added enjoyment, eat with chopsticks. Chew each bite thoroughly to appreciate the rich nutty flavor of the rice.

Cooking Schedule: Rice requires 45 minutes to cook and an additional 10 to 15 minutes to combine with vegetables. Rice can be made just before dinner, a few hours ahead and left covered at room temperature, or up to 3 days in advance and kept refrigerated until needed.

Prepare vegetables while rice cooks.

Salad and dressing can also be made while rice cooks.

Allow tea to steep while combining rice and vegetables.

A surprisingly substantial dish reminiscent of Chinese fried rice. It's a meal in itself.

FRIED BROWN RICE AND VEGETABLES

Utensils: covered saucepan; large skillet
Yield: 4 servings[1]
Preparation time: 10 minutes[2]
Cooking time: 1 hour[3]

2 *cups raw brown rice*
4 *cups water*
3 *cups mixed vegetables*[4]
Salt

1 *tablespoon oil*
Tamari Soy Sauce[5]
Handful of pine nuts

[1] To prepare for more (or less) people, allow ½ cup rice, 1 cup water and ¾ cup vegetables per serving.

[2] Preparation to be done simultaneously with cooking.

[3] If rice is already cooked cut cooking time down to 15 minutes.

[4] Choose vegetables according to taste. I highly recommend carrots and plenty of scallions plus any combination of the following: mushrooms, string beans, zucchini, corn, green peas, celery, beans, bean sprouts, and a little shredded lettuce or spinach.

[5] Tamari Soy Sauce is a type with only whole wheat flour, salt, and water added. It is sold in all health food stores. If you cannot find it, substi-

Wash rice in cold water and drain. Place in pot with cover. Add water. Bring to boil. Reduce heat, cover and cook over low flame 40 to 45 minutes, until water is completely absorbed. If grains are still hard, add additional ¼ cup water, cover and return to heat until water is absorbed. Remove from heat and lift cover partially to dry. While rice cooks wash desired vegetables and cut into ¼-inch pieces. Salt well. Heat oil over medium flame to cover bottom of skillet. Add one quarter of the rice. Sprinkle well with Tamari and add one quarter of the vegetables. Cook until vegetables are crisp-tender, 3 to 5 minutes. Push to side of skillet; add more rice, Tamari, and vegetables. Continue in this manner until all the rice and vegetables have been cooked.

Add pine nuts and stir once to mix all ingredients. Serve with additional Tamari soy sauce. This dish can be reheated as necessary. tute pure soy sauce to which no flavorings, colorings or artificial ingredients have been added.

Here is an unusual dressing of ground nuts and carrots passed on from a friend . . . made for those who like garlic. Add the optional yoghurt for a creamier version.

CABBAGE SALAD WITH CARROT DRESSING

Utensils: blender
Yield: 4 servings

1 small or ½ large head
   cabbage
½ cup peanut oil
1 carrot, diced
1 tablespoon sesame seeds

10 peanuts (20 if shelled)
1 clove garlic
2 teaspoons Tamari Soy Sauce
¼ cup yoghurt, optional

Shred or chop cabbage into bite-size pieces. Combine oil, carrot, sesame seeds, shelled peanuts, garlic, and soy sauce in blender container and process until smooth. Stir in yoghurt if desired and spoon over cabbage.

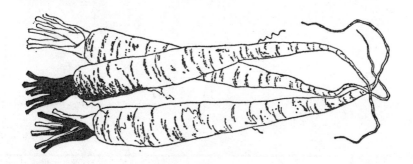

JAPANESE TEA

Bring water to a rapid boil. Place 1 teaspoon Mu, Bancha, or green tea for each cup of water in ceramic tea pot. Pour in boiling water and allow to steep at least 5 minutes. Serve in small cups throughout the meal. Do not reboil water once tea leaves have been added. This will release tannic acid and bring about a bitter flavor. Serve tea plain, without sugar or cream.

Menu ♯6

ARTICHOKE WITH CREAMY LEMON BUTTER
CHEESE SOUFFLÉ
GREEN BEANS WITH ALMONDS
DILLED TOMATOES

Serving Suggestions: Despite rumors to the contrary, a soufflé is one of the easiest dishes to prepare and takes only a few minutes to assemble. Although an elegant meal for company, this soufflé dinner is so easy to prepare you'll want to serve it for casual dining as well.

Serve the artichokes during the last 10 minutes the soufflé is in the oven.

Cooking Schedule: 55 minutes before dinner, start preparing the artichokes. When they begin to cook start the soufflé. If you're making the soufflé for 4 to 6 people it will have to go into the oven 30 to 45 minutes before you want to serve it; for 2 to 3, baking time is 20 to 30 minutes; and for individual soufflé dishes 15 to 20 minutes. So, time yourself accordingly, so soufflé can be served as soon as it's done. Directions for preparing the soufflé mixture and holding it until baking time are given in the recipe.

About 25 minutes before the soufflé is to be served prepare the beans. Then prepare the lemon butter. The tomatoes can be done at any time and take only a minute or two.

Artichokes make an impressive first course or salad and can be served hot or cold with lemon butter or your favorite French dressing. To eat artichokes, pull off individual leaf, dip in sauce, and pull through teeth, scraping off pulp; discard leaf. The small leaves in the center can be discarded but don't neglect the solid center or heart attached to the stem. Scrape off the attached leaves, pour on sauce, and eat with a fork. Sheer ecstasy!

ARTICHOKES

Utensils: large pot or Dutch oven
Yield: 4 servings
Preparation time: 10 minutes
Cooking time: 45 minutes

> *4 artichokes*
> *1 tablespoon lemon juice*
> *1 teaspoon salt*

[1] If artichokes are to be held before cooking place in large bowl with cold water and 1 tablespoon lemon juice to prevent discoloration. Prepare as close to cooking time as possible.

Trim stem of each artichoke to about ¼-inch long and remove tough leaves at base. Snip off sharp points at tip of each leaf with scissors.[1] Place trimmed artichokes in large pot with water to cover. Add lemon juice and salt. Bring to boil and cook, uncovered, about 45 minutes, until leaves can be pulled easily from the base and the stem end is fork-tender. Remove from water and turn upside down to drain.

If you're in a rush simply mix lemon juice with melted butter for a tasty sauce. But, if you're willing to spend a few minutes and have a sturdy arm the creamy version is a real delicacy.

CREAMY LEMON BUTTER

Utensils: wire whip
Yield: 1 cup
Preparation time: about 10 minutes

¼ cup lemon juice
¼ teaspoon salt
1 cup butter, divided into tablespoons

Boil lemon juice in small saucepan until 2 tablespoons remain. Remove from heat and add 1 tablespoon butter and beat with wire whip until melted. Repeat with second tablespoon butter. Place over very low heat and continue to add butter, 1 tablespoon at a time, beating well after each addition, until butter is melted and mixture is creamy.

The only part of the myth of soufflés that rings true is the delicate, creamy taste. Loud noises and bad vibrations won't make it fall. To show off your expertise serve as soon as it comes from the oven —it does fall as it cools. But, so what! The taste won't be altered a bit, so if it begins to droop ignore it—so will everyone else once they've had a taste.

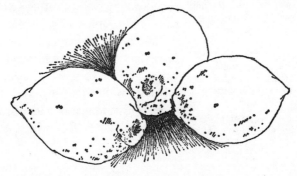

CHEESE SOUFFLÉ

Utensils: 1¾-quart soufflé dish or any deep baking dish with straight sides[2]; beater or wire whip
Yield: 4 to 6 servings[3]
Preparation time: 10 minutes
Baking time: 30 to 45 minutes[4]
Oven temperature: 375° F.

3 *tablespoons butter*	½ *teaspoon dry mustard*
3 *tablespoons potato starch*	6 *eggs, separated*[5]
1½ *cups milk*	2 *cups plus* 1½ *tablespoons*
½ *teaspoon salt*	*freshly grated cheese* (½
¼ *teaspoon pepper*	*Swiss and* ½ *Parmesan*)[6]
¼ *teaspoon nutmeg*	

[2] Depth and straight sides are essential for soufflé to rise properly. If soufflé for 2 is being made use a 1-quart casserole or soufflé dish. Or you can use small, individual soufflé dishes.

[3] For 2 to 3 servings divide all ingredients in half.

[4] For a soft creamy center which acts as a sauce for the soufflé cook minimum time —this is the French way. For a firmer soufflé with a uniform texture cook maximum time. Bake 1-quart soufflé 20 to 30 minutes; individual soufflés 15 to 20 minutes.

[5] It is easiest to separate eggs when they are cold so do this

Melt butter over low heat. Remove from heat and stir in potato starch to a smooth paste. Stir in milk, return to low heat and cook, stirring gently, until mixture thickens and comes to a boil. Remove from heat immediately.[7] Stir in seasonings and the 2 cups cheese, a small amount at a time, until cheese is melted. Cool slightly. Add egg yolks, one at a time, beating well.[8] Beat egg whites until stiff peaks form.[9] Mix a small amount of the beaten egg white (whatever clings to beaters) into cheese mixture to loosen batter and make mixing easier. Pour remaining whites on top and fold into cheese mixture gently with wire whip or rubber spatula.[10] Egg whites should be dispersed throughout but mixture need not be uniformly smooth. Do not over mix—this will reduce final volume. Grease the baking dish and shake the remaining cheese over inside to coat. Turn soufflé into prepared dish and bake in 375° F. oven 30 to 45 minutes. Serve immediately. Spoon from baking dish to serve.

as soon as eggs are removed from refrigerator. Egg whites obtain more volume when beaten at room temperature so let them stand out of the refrigerator after eggs have been separated.

6 To save time grate cheese in blender.

7 To substitute cornstarch or flour for potato starch to thicken sauce see directions for Cheese Sauce (see Index).

8 If desired, mixture can be chilled at this point until 5 minutes before baking time. If too thick to incorporate egg whites heat gently to thin.

9 The beaten egg whites cause the soufflé to rise. Beat with electric beater or wire whip until stiff peaks form—when beater is pulled out egg whites will stand in peaks and beater drawn through will leave groove. Do not overbeat.

10 To fold in egg whites: with rubber spatula cut through layer of whites to cheese mixture and bring cheese mixture over whites. Repeat several times until whites are evenly distributed throughout mixture.

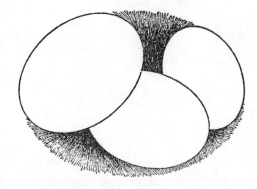

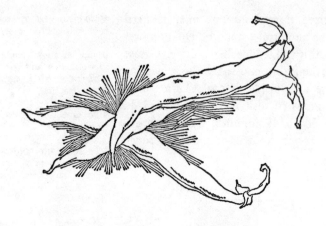

GREEN BEANS WITH ALMONDS

Yield: 4 servings
Preparation time: 5 minutes
Cooking time: 15 to 20 minutes

1 pound green beans
½ teaspoon salt

¼ cup water
¼ cup chopped almonds

Wash and trim ends of beans. Leave whole or break in half. Place in saucepan with salt and water. Bring to boil, cover, reduce heat and cook until tender but crunchy, about 15 minutes. Sprinkle with almonds just before serving.

DILLED TOMATOES

Slice tomatoes and sprinkle with lots of fresh chopped dill and ground pepper.

Menu #7

Cooking Schedule: Bread Sticks can be prepared at any time and stored indefinitely in a covered tin. Allow 20 minutes to assemble and 40 minutes baking time.

Tomato Sauce for the Eggplant Parmesan can be prepared ahead and stored in the refrigerator 1 week, the freezer 3 to 6 months. You can prepare several pints at one time and keep them for future meals. If desired, sauce can be prepared immediately before dinner. Begin 50 minutes before you want to put the eggplant in the oven, or 1 hour and 10 minutes before dinner.

Begin preparing eggplant 35 minutes before dinner, or 10 to 15 minutes before putting it in the oven. This dish can be prepared earlier in the day and kept in the refrigerator until baking time. Preparation of the eggplant can take place while sauce simmers.

Salad, dressing, and juice can be prepared while eggplant bakes.

Whole wheat bread sticks are available commercially, but if you have the time they are nice to make at home. They store for months.

WHOLE WHEAT BREAD STICKS

Utensils: baking sheet
Yield: 60 bread sticks
Preparation time: 20 minutes
Baking time: 40 minutes
Oven temperature: 350° F.

2 cups wheat germ
2 cups whole wheat flour
1¼ cups milk[1]
½ cup oil

1 tablespoon honey
1 teaspoon salt
Sesame seeds

[1] Reconstituted dry milk powder works well here and is a great money saver in baking. Prepare 1¼ cups following package directions.

Mix together ingredients in large bowl. Then, knead on oilcloth or well floured surface, hands covered with flour to prevent sticking, until dough is easy to handle. Take a small amount of dough and roll in the palm of your hand, like a rope or coil, to form sticks ¼ inch thick and 5 inches long. Roll in sesame seeds and place on well greased baking sheet. Continue until all dough is used. Bake in 350° F. oven 40 minutes. Remove from baking sheet, cool and store.

Homemade Tomato Sauce can make a meal out of anything. A good time to prepare the sauce is 1) on a quiet evening at home, 2) while waiting for a loaf of bread to bake, 3) when tomatoes are plentiful or on sale, 4) when you're in the mood.

I always make several pints at once and keep them in the freezer so I'm never without.

BASIC TOMATO SAUCE

Utensils: large pot with lid; food mill or blender
Yield: 4 pints
Preparation time: 10 minutes
Cooking time: 1 hour

1 tablespoon oil	15 medium tomatoes
1 onion, sliced	1 teaspoon salt
4 small Italian peppers[2]	¼ teaspoon pepper

[2] If you cannot find Italian peppers substitute 1 green pepper for every 2 Italian.

[3] After tomatoes have been cooked skins slip off easily, it just takes time to fish them out. Puréeing the sauce in a food mill makes this easier. This is not an essential step, the sauce will just be more uniformly smooth without the skins. It all depends on your own preference, so try it both ways and decide for yourself.

[4] For Italian Sauce (for 6 cups sauce before cooking down or half the recipe): add 2 cloves crushed garlic, 2 tablespoons dried basil, 1 tablespoon each oregano and thyme, 1 teaspoon salt, and, if desired, 1 bunch snipped parsley. It's a good idea to use the other half of the batch for Plain Tomato Sauce (add 1 teaspoon salt only before cooking down) or Mexican Sauce (see Index).

Heat oil in large pot. Add onion and cook 2 to 3 minutes, until tender and transparent. While onion cooks slice peppers. Add sliced pepper to pot, cover, and cook over low heat while you cut tomatoes. Remove core from tomatoes and cut into eighths. Add to pot, cover, and cook gently 10 minutes, until liquid begins to separate from tomatoes. Stir, add salt and pepper, cover, and cook over low heat an additional 15 to 20 minutes, until soft. Remove from heat. If desired remove skins.[3] Purée in food mill or pour into blender container and process at low speed until smooth. Sauce will be fairly thin and measure 10 to 12 cups. Return to pot, season as desired,[4] and cook, uncovered, about 30 minutes, until thickened and reduced to 8 cups. To store, pour into pint containers leaving ¼ inch at top, cool, cover, and freeze.

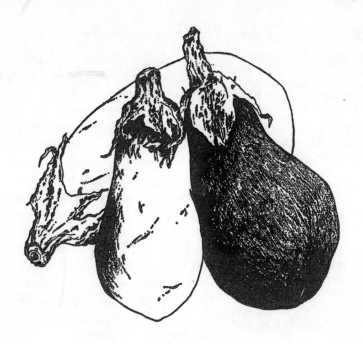

There are endless versions of this dish. I prefer this one—it's not all breading like most and gets its substance from the creamy melted cheese throughout.

EGGPLANT PARMESAN

Utensils: 2 quart casserole or baking dish[5]
Yield: 4 servings[6]
Preparation time: 10 to 15 minutes
Baking time: 15 to 20 minutes
Oven temperature: 350° F.

2 small or 1 large eggplant
Oil
½ pound mozzarella cheese,
   thinly sliced

2 cups (1 pint) Italian
   Tomato Sauce (above)
Grated Parmesan cheese[7]

[5] A deep casserole produces a thicker, creamier, multilayered dish; a shallow casserole gives fewer layers and a crustier top. Take your pick.

[6] This recipe can easily be adjusted for additional servings. Add 1 small eggplant, ¼ pound mozzarella cheese, and ½ to 1 cup sauce for each 2 servings.

[7] Use freshly grated Parmesan cheese only. Keep refrigerated until just before grating to make the job easier and use a blender if you like, although for small quantities a hand grater will be just as quick.

[8] As an alternative to broiling, the eggplant slices can be sautéed in hot oil until lightly browned, however, this method takes longer since all the slices can't be fried simultaneously. If you use this method, remember eggplant absorbs oil like a sponge. As you continue to fry slices add oil only as necessary to prevent sticking.

[9] At this point the casserole can be refrigerated for several hours if you like to work ahead. Remove from refrigerator and allow to come to room temperature before baking or increase baking time 5 to 10 minutes.

Wash eggplant; do not peel. Trim ends and cut eggplant crosswise into slices ¼ inch thick. Place on broiler pan or rack, brush surface with oil, and broil about 3 inches from heat 5 minutes, until lightly browned. Turn, brush uncooked side with oil, and broil 3 minutes on other side.[8] Place single layer of cooked eggplant slices on bottom of casserole. Cover with single layer of mozzarella cheese, spoon over enough sauce to cover, and sprinkle generously with grated Parmesan. Repeat layers until all eggplant is used, adding the Parmesan cheese layer every other time. End with tomato sauce and Parmesan cheese. Any extra sauce can be poured over top layer if needed for moisture and will filter down during baking.[9] Bake in 350° F. oven 15 to 20 minutes, until sauce bubbles and cheese melts. Serve from casserole with large cooking spoon, cutting cheese strands with scissors.

ITALIAN SALAD

Prepare salad for desired number using shredded lettuce, romaine, tomato wedges, raw cauliflower buds, and olives, if desired. To make dressing, chop 1 clove garlic; mix garlic, ¾ cup olive oil, ½ cup wine vinegar, ½ teaspoon salt, ¼ teaspoon ground pepper, and a pinch of oregano. Shake well before pouring. For variety add 2 tablespoons finely grated Parmesan cheese.

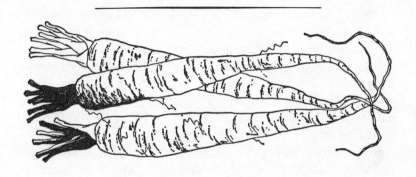

APPLE-CARROT JUICE

For every two servings measure 1 cup apple cider or unsweetened apple juice into blender container. Add 1 carrot which has been peeled if necessary and cut into pieces. Blend at high speed until smooth and foamy. Serve immediately over ice.

Menu #8

VEGETABLE CHOPPED LIVER
POTATO PANCAKES
APPLESAUCE
STUFFED PRUNES

Serving Suggestions: Serve dinner just after pancakes are cooked to insure maximum crispness.

Cooking Schedule: Prepare Vegetable Chopped Liver a day ahead or early in the morning so it can chill. Allow 30 minutes for cooking and assembling. Keeps 4 to 5 days in the refrigerator.

Two variations are given for the Applesauce. The cooked version takes about 30 minutes from start to finish, can be served warm, at room temperature, or chilled. It keeps several weeks in the refrigerator. The quick version takes about 2 minutes to make and should be served soon after. Try both.

If the prunes have pits, soak them while preparing the Potato Pancakes. Stuff prunes while pancakes cook. Begin both operations about 25 minutes before dinner. Pancakes should be prepared just before cooking to prevent discoloration.

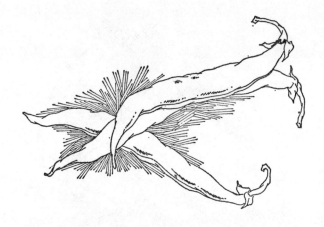

This purée of green beans, onions, and egg looks and tastes like chopped calf's liver. Serve as an appetizer or hors d'oeuvre on whole wheat crackers. Also makes a hearty sandwich with lettuce on pumpernickel.

VEGETABLE CHOPPED LIVER

Yield: 2 cups
Preparation time: 30 minutes

¾ to 1 *pound green beans*
Boiling water
2 *tablespoons oil*
1 *onion, chopped*

1 *hard-cooked egg*
½ *teaspoon salt*
⅛ *teaspoon pepper*

Trim beans and cook, covered, in small amount of boiling water until tender, about 20 minutes. Heat oil and brown onion lightly. Drain beans and chop finely or grind. Mash hard-cooked egg with beans, blend in onion, salt, and pepper to form a compact mass. Chill. Add additional salt and pepper if necessary to taste.

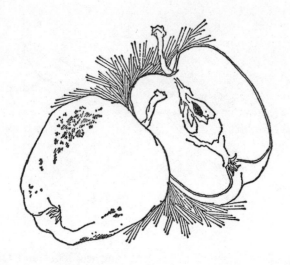

Here are two versions of applesauce. The first is a rich, cooked sauce that calls for a few extra minutes before dinner, but stores well. The second is ideal for quick service, retains the maximum amount of vitamins, but should be used immediately. The uncooked version will turn dark on standing. A little lemon juice can be added to retard the browning.

COOKED APPLESAUCE

Utensils: large pot with cover; food mill
Yield: about 5 cups
Preparation time: 5 to 10 minutes
Cooking time: 20 minutes

> 2 pounds apples[1]
> ¼ cup water
> 6 cloves

> ½ teaspoon cinnamon,
> optional
> ¼ teaspoon nutmeg, optional

[1] Use sweet apples. If using green apples or other tart variety sweeten sauce with honey to taste.

Dice apples. No need to pare or core. Place in large saucepan, add water and cloves, cover, and cook over low heat

15 to 20 minutes, until tender. Shake pot
from time to time to prevent sticking. If
necessary add additional water. Remove
cloves and purée in food mill. Discard
skins, core, and seeds. Cool. If desired,
add cinnamon and nutmeg to puréed apples and cook briefly before cooling.

INSTANT APPLESAUCE

Utensils: blender
Yield: 4 servings

> 1 *pound (3 medium) apples*
> *Apple juice or cider*

Core apples and dice; do not peel. Purée in blender, a few pieces
of apple at a time and just enough cider to blend, adding more
apple as it blends and additional juice as needed. Vary by adding
a few ripe strawberries or a diced banana.

A garnish to the meal that is nutritious and perfect for snacks as
well.

STUFFED PRUNES

Yield: 4 servings

Use pitted prunes or soak 8 to 12 prunes with pits in warm water
10 to 20 minutes to soften. Slit top of prune and slip out pit. Stuff
hollow center with ½ teaspoon peanut butter.

If you like your pancakes crisp make them thin and fry quickly. For a crisp outside and a chewy center use more batter for each pancake.

POTATO PANCAKES

Utensils: Blender or coarse grater; large skillet
Yield: 4 servings
Preparation time: 10 minutes
Cooking time: about 15 minutes

2 *eggs*
3 *cups peeled grated potatoes, well drained (about 7 medium potatoes)*[2]
1 *small onion, grated*

1 *teaspoon salt*
¼ *teaspoon pepper*
About 2 *tablespoons whole wheat cracker crumbs*[3]
About ½ *cup oil*

[2] To grate potatoes in electric blender place a few pieces diced potato in container with just enough water to start machine. Drain well and add a few more pieces with water. Be sure to drain potatoes as thoroughly as possible before adding to other ingredients. Prepare just prior to cooking or potatoes will darken.

[3] If batter is too loose add additional cracker crumbs.

[4] Cooked pancakes can be kept warm in a low oven. They will loose some crispness on standing.

Beat eggs. Add potatoes, onion, salt, pepper, and cracker crumbs. Heat a ¼-inch layer of oil in skillet. Drop potato mixture by spoonfuls into hot fat. Fry crisp on both sides. Add more oil to pan as necessary. Drain cooked pancakes on absorbent paper and serve immediately.[4]

Menu #9

BROILED GRAPEFRUIT
SPINACH SALAD
WHOLE GRAIN PUMPERNICKEL

Serving Suggestions: A good, quick meal which can be made for any number of people.

Cooking Schedule: Hard-cooked eggs used here are best chilled. It's a good idea to keep several on hand in the refrigerator for making egg salad, snacking, and use in salads.

This meal takes only minutes to prepare.

Raw spinach is an excellent salad base alone or combined with other greens. Ingredients can be varied as whim, or your refrigerator, dictates.

SPINACH SALAD

Yield: 4 servings
Preparation time: 10 minutes

1 pound raw spinach
¼ pound raw mushrooms
4 scallions
16 cherry tomatoes

¼ pound feta cheese
4 hard-cooked eggs
French Dressing (recipe follows)

Wash spinach, discard tough stems and tear remaining stems and leaves into bite-size pieces. Divide evenly among four large salad dishes or soup bowls. Slice scallions thinly; wash mushrooms and slice lengthwise into thin pieces; halve each tomato. Divide ingredients equally and add to each bowl; toss. Crumble one-quarter of the cheese on top of each salad. Top with sliced egg. Pour dressing over all.

FRENCH DRESSING

Measure ⅔ cup oil and ⅓ cup vinegar into jar with cover. Add ½ teaspoon dry mustard, ¼ teaspoon paprika, and ½ teaspoon salt. Cover and shake. Pour immediately or store in refrigerator until needed. Shake well before pouring. Serve chilled grapefruit halves or vary them this way:

BROILED GRAPEFRUIT

Allow ½ grapefruit per person. Cut grapefruit in half crosswise. Remove core and cut around each section loosening fruit from membrane, if desired. Cover cut surface with thin coating of honey. Place under broiler heat about 5 minutes, until surface begins to brown and bubble. Serve immediately.

WHOLE GRAIN PUMPERNICKEL

Purchase in health food store or check local grocery for whole grain black bread, often called "Old World" or "Country Style" pumpernickel. Look for brands which don't contain calcium propionate, added to retard spoilage. Keeps well for at least 2 weeks in refrigerator.

Menu #10

GUACAMOLE
CHEESE ENCHILADAS
MEXICAN BEANS
SHREDDED LETTUCE

Serving Suggestions: Best when friends are expected. Very impressive and worth the time.

Cooking Schedule: There are a number of ways to approach this meal. To begin everything before dinner can be quite confusing, but much of the preparation can be done ahead if you plan in advance (and, this is one meal worth the forethought).

The sauce can be prepared and stored up to 3 months in the freezer or a week in the refrigerator. It is made from the Basic Tomato Sauce and requires about 50 minutes to cook up. The beans can be cooked in advance and stored in the refrigerator for at least 1 week. Final preparation of the beans is 15 minutes and can take place just before you sit down to dinner—while the enchiladas are in the oven.

It is best to prepare the enchiladas in stages. First, the tortillas. This takes 35 to 45 minutes and can be done a day ahead or in the morning. If you like you can assemble the enchiladas immediately and refrigerate or assemble them any time up to 10 minutes before serving time. Allow about 15 minutes to assemble.

Guacamole takes 5 minutes to put together and can be done before you begin the final preparation for the meal and refrigerated until serving time. Do not prepare Guacamole more than 1 hour in advance.

With the sauce, tortillas and beans cooked, organize your time as follows for an easy meal: 1) 30 minutes before dinner prepare Guacamole, 2) then assemble enchiladas, 3) prepare all ingredients for beans, place enchiladas in the oven and finish beans.

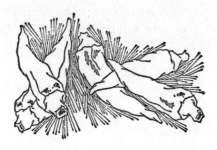

Here are the directions for preparing a spicy Mexican Hot Sauce from our Basic Tomato Sauce recipe. The recipe given here calls for half the initial batch of sauce (6 cups reduced to 4 in cooking). To make enchiladas for 4 you'll use 1 pint (2 cups) of this sauce. If you don't like your Mexican food good and spicy, cut down on the chilies, but give this version a try at least once.

MEXICAN HOT SAUCE

Yield: 2 pints
Preparation time: 5 minutes
Cooking time: 20 minutes

*Basic Tomato Sauce, ½
    recipe (6 cups) (see
    Index)*

*3 chili peppers[1]
¼ teaspoon ground coriander
1 teaspoon salt*

Wash chilies and chop. Be careful not to touch the seeds as they are very hot and will burn the skin.[2] Add chopped chilies, coriander and salt to Basic Tomato Sauce and cook, uncovered, over medium heat 20 minutes, until slightly thickened and reduced to about 4 cups. Store as you would Basic Tomato Sauce.[3]

[1] If fresh hot chili peppers are not available substitute 2 tablespoons chili powder.

[2] It is wise to wear gloves when handling fresh chilies.

[3] Follow storing instructions for Basic Tomato Sauce (see Index).

Tortillas, thin corn meal cakes, are the Mexican counterpart of bread. Although they take a little time to make they are actually quite easy to do.

TORTILLAS

Utensils: rolling pin; 1 or 2 skillets or griddle
Yield: about 12 tortillas[4]
Preparation time: 20 minutes
Cooking time: 2 to 3 minutes each. Preparation and cooking time can overlap, requiring 35 to 45 minutes total

1 cup corn flour or finely ground corn meal ½ cup whole wheat flour	1 teaspoon salt 10 to 12 tablespoons warm water

[4] You will probably get 1 or 2 extra tortillas from the dough. This way you can choose the best.

[5] To speed cooking process use 2 skillets. Roll dough as some of the tortillas cook and cook as many at a time as skillet can accommodate.

Mix corn flour, whole wheat flour and salt. Stir in water with fork until dough holds together when pressed with fingers. Add the last 2 tablespoons water only if needed. Form 12 small balls, using 1 rounded tablespoon dough for each. Flatten each ball slightly and place on board or oilcloth dusted with corn flour. Cover with sheet of oiled or waxed paper and roll in all directions to make a thin pancake about 5 inches in diameter. Lift paper; slide a long thin knife under pancake to loosen from board. Place on hot, ungreased griddle or skillet and cook over medium heat until lightly browned, about 2 minutes. Turn and cook 1 minute on other side. Continue using all dough.[5] Store cooked tortillas several hours or overnight in plastic bag.

A wonderful Mexican invention of rolled Tortillas with a melted cheese filling and a spicy tomato sauce.

CHEESE ENCHILADAS

Utensils: large shallow baking dish
Yield: 4 servings
Preparation time: 15 minutes
Baking time: 10 minutes
Oven temperature: 350° F.

2 cups Mexican Hot Sauce (above)
12 Tortillas

2 cups (½ pound) grated Monterey Jack Cheese[6]
1 small onion, chopped

Heat sauce to boiling point.[7] Dip cooked tortilla in heated sauce briefly, until pliable. Place 2 tablespoons cheese and 1 tablespoon onion on tortilla and roll. Place seam side down in baking dish. Continue until all tortillas and filling are used. Spoon remaining sauce over rolled enchiladas. Bake, uncovered, in 350° F. oven 10 minutes until cheese melts. Or, cover and refrigerate until baking time, allowing 15 minutes to heat through. Leftovers can be refrigerated and reheated.

[6] If Monterey Jack cheese is not available substitute natural munster. For ease grate in blender.

[7] Save time and grate cheese and chop onion while sauce heats.

Guacamole is an avocado dish that can be served before the meal as a dip (with whole wheat crackers or leftover tortillas) or along with the meal as a salad.

GUACAMOLE

Yield: 4 servings
Preparation time: 5 minutes

1 *clove garlic*	½ *teaspoon salt*
1 *large or 2 small avocados*	¼ *teaspoon pepper sauce*[8]
1 *tablespoon lemon juice*	
1 *small or ½ large tomato,*	
finely chopped	

[8] If you like your food hot increase pepper sauce to taste.

[9] Avocado turns brown when exposed to air. The lemon juice and the pit help prevent browning. Guacamole should be made within 1 hour of serving.

Cut garlic in half and rub bowl well with cut surface. Peel avocado and mash, in serving bowl, with fork. Reserve pit. Sprinkle lemon juice over mashed avocado and add remaining ingredients. Mix well. Serve immediately or place pit in center, cover, and refrigerate until serving time.[9]

Kidney beans are prepared in an unusual way here—half mashed and spicy, the other half whole and lightly sweetened. Either way is delicious alone, and together they give an interesting taste and texture combination.

MEXICAN BEANS

Utensils: small saucepan and skillet
Yield: 4 servings
Preparation time: 5 minutes
Cooking time: 10 minutes

About 2¾ cups cooked
  kidney beans[10]
2 tablespoons cooking liquid
  from beans
1 tablespoon molasses
2 tablespoons oil
½ onion, chopped
2 teaspoons chili powder

Divide beans in half. Place one half in small saucepan, add cooking liquid and molasses and cook over medium heat until dry. Meanwhile heat oil in skillet and cook onion until lightly browned. Add remaining beans and mash with fork or potato masher. Add chili powder, mix and fry over high heat until dry. To serve place ¼ mashed beans on each plate and top with cooked whole beans.

[10] For cooked beans, soak 1 cup dried kidney beans in 3 cups water overnight or bring to boil in water for 2 minutes, remove from heat, cover, and let stand at least 1 hour. After soaking, cook, covered, over low heat 1 hour. Add 2 teaspoons salt and cook, covered, ½ hour longer, or until tender.

SHREDDED LETTUCE

Shred lettuce just before serving and place alongside the Enchiladas on each plate. The shredded lettuce cuts the spiciness of the other dishes and refreshes the palate.

Menu #11

Serving Suggestions: This Dinner Loaf is a unique dish that you might enjoy introducing into the diet of others. A word of warning: it is spinach-green throughout, so if your friends are funny about the color of their food, save it for someone who'll appreciate the wonderful taste.

Serve the Fruit Cup while the loaf is cooling.

Cooking Schedule: Begin the Dinner Loaf 1 hour and 20 minutes before dinner. During the last hour the loaf will be in the oven and the rest of the dinner can be prepared.

If you are making this for company and find it easier to work ahead, you can prepare the loaf earlier and reheat briefly in a 300° F. oven until warm, or serve it at room temperature. In this case only the carrots need wait until the last minute to be made.

To repeat, the loaf is green, but don't let that disarm you. The appearance, except for the color, is of a meat loaf, the flavor is "indescribably delicious," and it is excellent warm or at room temperature. The cold mayonnaise sauce is the perfect taste complement.

DINNER LOAF

Utensils: blender; 9×5×3-inch loaf pan
Yield: 6 servings
Preparation time: 20 minutes
Baking time: 55 minutes
Oven temperature: 350° F.

1 tablespoon oil
1 onion, chopped
1 cup cracked wheat[1]
2 cups water
2 teaspoons salt
1 pound spinach (about 2
    cups cooked)

1 cup unsalted peanuts
2 eggs
1/4 teaspoon pepper or 1/2
    teaspoon pepper sauce

Heat oil in small saucepan and sauté onion and cracked wheat until onion is transparent. Add water and 1/2 teaspoon salt. Bring to boil, cover, reduce heat, and cook over very low heat until water is absorbed, 15 minutes. Wash spinach and cook in water that clings to the leaves in a covered pot, 5 minutes, until wilted. Place spinach, peanuts, and 1 egg in blender and process at high speed until creamed. It may be necessary to turn blender on and off and push contents

[1] Cracked wheat is also referred to as bulghur or wheat pilaf.

[2] If you wish pan can be lined with oiled foil to facilitate removal of loaf.

[3] Allow slices to cool slightly before serving for richest flavor.

down with a rubber spatula at first. When mixture can be blended without stopping machine it is ready. Lightly beat the remaining egg and combine it with the spinach mixture, cooked cracked wheat, remaining 1½ teaspoons salt, and the pepper. Turn into a well oiled[2] 9×5× 3-inch loaf pan. Bake in 350° F. oven 55 minutes. Cool in pan 5 to 10 minutes to set the loaf. Cut in slices to serve.[3]

The Green Mayonnaise is used to garnish the individual slices of Dinner Loaf. Place a small amount on each slice and serve the remainder in a bowl so everyone can help themselves to more.

GREEN MAYONNAISE[4]

Utensils: blender
Yield: about 1 cup
Preparation time: 5 minutes

1 egg
2 tablespoons lemon juice
½ teaspoon salt

½ teaspoon dry mustard
1 cup peanut oil
¼ cup chopped parsley

[4] You can use previously prepared mayonnaise, adding lemon juice and parsley, as a substitute.

Combine egg, lemon juice, salt, and mustard in blender. Add ¼ cup oil, turn blender to high, and process, immediately pouring in remaining oil in a slow steady stream until blended. Stir in parsley and chill until needed.

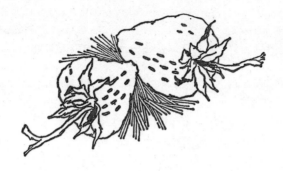

FRESH FRUIT CUP

Yield: 6 servings
Preparation time: about 15 minutes; varies with skill

3 oranges, peeled and
    sectioned[5]
2 apples, diced
1 banana, sliced

12 strawberries, halved
½ to 1 cup diced pineapple
12 dried dates, chopped

Cut all fruit over bowl to retain all liquid. Mix fruit and liquid together and chill. If more liquid is desired add orange juice, apple juice, or a thin mixture of any fresh fruit juices on hand. Remove from refrigerator a few minutes before serving to develop fruit flavors.[6]

[5] To prepare orange cut a thin slice from top. Cut off peel round and round spiral fashion, removing white membrane without cutting into fruit. Go over fruit again, removing any remaining white membrane. Cut along side of each dividing membrane from outside to middle of fruit. Remove section by section. Prepare fruit over a bowl.

[6] Fruits can be varied to please taste and budget. Halved pecans are also a suggested addition to the mélange.

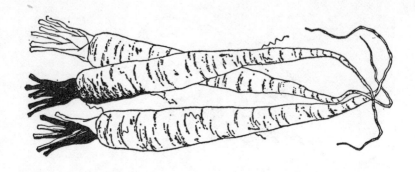

A sweet vegetable dish which can also be made with onion slices, turnips, parsnips or apple rings.

GLAZED CARROTS

Yield: 6 servings
Cooking time: 20 to 25 minutes

1½ *bunches carrots*	3 *tablespoons butter*
Boiling *water*	
3 *tablespoons molasses or*	
honey	

Peel carrots if necessary. Cut crosswise into nuggets or coins and place in small amount of boiling salted water. Cover and cook over medium heat until almost tender, about 10 minutes. Drain. Heat molasses and butter; add carrots and cook gently, about 15 minutes, until coated. Turn carrots and baste occasionally.

Menu #12

BROCCOLI WITH CHEESE SAUCE
ORANGE-DATE SALAD
OATMEAL BREAD

Serving Suggestions: You'll be amazed how satisfying this meal is. It's another one to keep in mind when you don't want to fuss.

Cooking Schedule: Prepare bread early in the day or take a previously made loaf from the freezer to thaw. Bread takes 3 hours from start to finish and this includes 1 hour and 45 minutes rising time and 45 to 50 minutes baking time.

Begin the rest of the meal 20 minutes before serving time. Prepare the ingredients for the salad first. Then put the broccoli up to cook and make the sauce. Just before serving put the salad together.

A compact loaf of bread with a mildly sweet, delicate flavor.

OATMEAL BREAD

Utensils: 2 8×4×2-inch loaf pans
Yield: 2 loaves
Preparation time: 20 minutes
Rising time: 1 hour and 45 minutes
Baking time: 45 to 50 minutes
Oven temperature: 350° F.

1 cup rolled oats
2 cups milk, heated to boiling
2 tablespoons dry yeast (2 packages)

Approximately 4½ cups whole wheat flour
¼ teaspoon ginger
2 teaspoons salt
½ cup molasses

[1] For instructions on kneading and addition of flour consult notes for Whole Wheat Rolls (see Index).

[2] To shape loaf: flatten a ball of dough, pressing into a rectangular shape. Fold in half lengthwise. Then stretch dough until it is about 3 times as long as baking pan. Fold into thirds to fit pan by overlapping ends at center. Now fold dough lengthwise so sides meet in center. Press edges down firmly to seal and roll the loaf gently to finish shaping. Place seam side down in pan.

Place oats in large bowl and pour in hot milk. Let stand until lukewarm. Meanwhile combine yeast, 2 cups flour, ginger and salt. Drain oats, reserving milk, and stir flour mixture into softened oats. Add reserved milk and molasses and stir well. Add additional flour to make a soft dough. Cover with clean cloth and set in warm place to rise until double in volume, or about 1 hour. Turn dough onto well floured board or oilcloth and knead, adding flour as necessary to prevent sticking, 5 to 10 minutes.[1] Divide dough in half and shape into 2 loaves.[2] Place loaves in 2 greased 8×4×2-inch loaf pans, cover with cloth and let rise until double in size, about 45 minutes. Bake in

350° F. oven 45 to 50 minutes.[3] Remove from pan immediately and cool on wire rack. Cool thoroughly before freezing.

[3] Bread is completely baked when it shrinks from sides of pan and sounds hollow when tapped.

ORANGE-DATE SALAD

For every two servings slice 8 dried dates, about ⅓ cup. Marinate dates in a French dressing made by combining 1 tablespoon lemon juice, 2½ tablespoons oil, ⅛ teaspoon salt, and ½ teaspoon honey. Peel and section 1 large orange. To serve, place orange sections on a bed of lettuce and pour over dates and dressing.

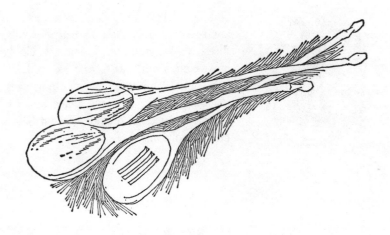

Whole cooked broccoli stalks with a creamy cheese sauce are a filling meal. Follow these basic directions and increase proportionately to provide as many servings as you need.

BROCCOLI

Utensils: large saucepan
Yield: 2 servings
Preparation time: 5 minutes
Cooking time: 15 minutes

[4] If stems are very thick slice lengthwise almost to buds to insure even cooking.

For every two servings wash 1 bunch broccoli and trim tough stem ends. Cut stalks so broccoli can stand upright in large pot. Slice trimmed-off portions of stalk into ½-inch-thick rounds. Heat to boiling enough water to reach just below broccoli buds. Add ½ teaspoon salt, sliced stalks, and whole stalks.[4] Cook, uncovered, 5 minutes. Cover, reduce heat, and cook 10 minutes longer. Drain well, reserving liquid. To serve, place on serving dish and pour on hot Cheese Sauce (recipe follows).

CHEESE SAUCE

Utensils: small saucepan
Yield: about 1½ cups sauce
Preparation time: 5 minutes
Cooking time: 5 minutes

1 tablespoon butter
1 tablespoon potato starch[5]
1 cup milk
½ teaspoon salt
¼ teaspoon pepper

¼ teaspoon nutmeg
1 cup (¼ pound) grated
   cheese[6]
¼ cup broccoli liquid

Melt butter in small saucepan. Add potato starch and stir to form a smooth paste. Remove from heat and stir in milk.[7] Return to low heat and cook, stirring constantly, until mixture thickens and reaches boiling point. Remove from heat immediately.[8] Add seasonings and grated cheese, stirring until melted and smooth. Return to low heat if necessary to melt cheese. Add hot broccoli liquid and stir smooth. Sauce can be reheated if necessary by stirring over low heat.

[5] Or, use equivalent thickener (see Index).

[6] Use Cheddar, natural munster, or Parmesan cheese to suit taste.

[7] For best results stir with wooden spoon or rubber spatula.

[8] If you use cornstarch or flour to thicken sauce allow to boil about 3 minutes to remove starchy taste. Bring potato starch only to boiling point—additional cooking will cause sauce to thin out.

Menu #13

GLADYS'S RICE AND BEAN STEW
GEORGE'S FRIED PLANTAINS
CABBAGE SLAW SALAD

Serving Suggestions: A good meal for a crowd—filling and easily prepared in advance and reheated, or held until you're ready.

Cooking Schedule: Beans need to be presoaked 1 hour before cooking begins. Like any stew slow cooking is the key to good flavor. Required cooking time is 2 hours here. Stew can easily be prepared in advance if desired and held at room temperature up to 2 hours or refrigerated for use the next day. During the first hour the beans are cooking the rest of the preparation can be done and will take about 15 minutes.

Prepare salad any time during last hour stew is cooking, allowing yourself 15 minutes. Salad can be served immediately after preparation or refrigerated until needed. The longer it stands the softer it becomes. It's delicious crunchy and it's delicious wilted.

Prepare plantains just before serving. Leave 10 minutes to prepare and cook.

Inspired by Puerto Rican cuisine, this is a hearty, delicately flavored stew. In France a similar dish is known as cassoulet, in Jewish cuisine, cholent.

GLADYS'S RICE AND BEAN STEW

Utensils: large pot with cover
Yield: 6 servings[1]
Preparation time: 15 minutes
Cooking time: 2 hours

½ *pound (1¼ cups) dried
    white beans*
4 *cups water*
2 *tablespoons oil*
1 *medium onion, chopped*
2 *tomatoes, chopped*
1 *green pepper, chopped*
1 *sweet Italian pepper,
    chopped[2]*
1 *large clove garlic, chopped*
1 *small acorn squash, peeled
    and cut in cubes*

2 *sprigs cilantro (fresh
    coriander) or Italian
    parsley*
1 *tablespoon salt*
1 *cup short grain brown
    rice*
1 *tablespoon capers*
¼ *teaspoon pepper sauce*

Place beans in large pot, add water and bring to boil 1 minute. Remove from heat, cover and let stand at least 1 hour. Return to heat and cook slowly over low heat until almost tender, 1 hour. Meanwhile, heat oil in skillet and cook onion, tomato, peppers, and garlic until tender, about 5 minutes. Measure liquid from cooked beans and add water if necessary to measure 3 cups. Add sautéed vege-

[1] For fewer servings divide all ingredients proportionately, i.e. for 2 servings divide all ingredients by 3.

[2] If Italian pepper is not available, substitute 1 sweet red pepper, chopped.

[3] If you prefer a thick stew let stand ½ hour before serving or cook until desired consistency. If you want stew to be an asopao (a soup-stew) you can add additional water when reheating. It may be necessary to add more water if you are preparing stew in advance or reheating leftovers.

tables and remaining ingredients to beans and liquid. Cover and cook over low heat until rice is tender, 1 hour. Remove from heat and let stand, covered, until ready to serve. As stew stands it will absorb most of the liquid.[3]

Serve the salad fresh and crunchy or marinate to wilt according to taste. Spicy and refreshing either way.

CABBAGE SLAW SALAD

Yield: 6 servings
Preparation time: 15 minutes

½ cabbage, chopped
2 small tomatoes, diced
3 ribs celery, chopped
3 tablespoons peanut oil

2 tablespoons cider vinegar
½ teaspoon salt
¼ teaspoon pepper sauce, or
    more to taste

Toss all ingredients together and refrigerate until serving time.

Plantains, a starchy variety of banana, look like large bananas. They are available in Spanish markets. They can be used green, or yellow and speckled for a sweeter, less starchy taste. If not available, substitute slightly green bananas.

GEORGE'S FRIED PLANTAINS

Allow 1 plantain for 2 to 3 people. Peel as a banana and slice diagonally for more surface area. Soak briefly in salted water to prevent darkening. Drain. Sauté over medium heat in skillet, adding oil as necessary to prevent sticking, until brown and crisp on both sides and tender in the middle. Drain on absorbent paper. Serve hot.

Menu #14

Serving Suggestions: Don't be thrown by the strange names and lengthy cooking schedule. If you plan your time according to directions the meal will be astonishingly easy to prepare. And, even if it weren't easy, it would be worth it!

Serve the Baba Ghannooj first with Pita or serve everything together, as you wish.

Cooking Schedule: Begin by cooking the dried chick peas. This means soaking overnight or 1 hour using the quick soak method and 1½ to 2 hours cooking time. This can be done days in advance.

The Baba Ghannooj is the next step and calls for 45 minutes initially to bake the eggplant. This can be done either while the beans cook earlier in the day or to be ready ½ hour before serving. It should have this ½ hour resting time after it is combined with the other ingredients so the garlic has a chance to penetrate.

If you're preparing the sauce from scratch (making your own tahini) use the time it takes to bake the eggplant to do this, as well as to make the Tabouli.

When you've finished the Baba assemble the Fallafel and fry immediately if you've planned your time to finish just before dinner, or chill uncooked Fallafel until 20 minutes before serving time.

The entire meal, from scratch to service, including the soaking of the beans takes 3½ hours. All the work can be done in advance, leaving only 20 minutes cooking time at the end. Once the beans are already cooked the meal can be prepared 1 hour and 15 minutes before serving time.

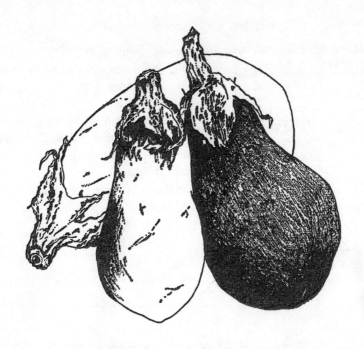

This Mideastern specialty is an eggplant dip with a distinct garlic taste. Everyone eats from a common bowl, dipping pieces of warmed pita bread into the purée.

BABA GHANNOOJ

Yield: 4 servings
Preparation time: 5 minutes
Baking time: 45 minutes[1]
Oven temperature: 375° F.

1 eggplant	3 tablespoons tahini[2]
1 teaspoon salt	1 to 2 tablespoons olive oil
2 cloves garlic, crushed	1/4 teaspoon ground cumin
1/4 cup lemon juice	

[1] If you prefer, eggplant can be speared on a long fork and held directly over a flame, turning frequently, until soft inside and charred outside, about 10 minutes. This imparts a fine charcoal taste to the dip.

[2] Tahini is a sesame seed paste available in Mideast groceries, health food and specialty stores. Tahini can be made at home as directed in the recipe which follows for Tahini Sauce.

[3] As tahini is added mixture will thicken and turn light.

Bake whole eggplant in 375° F. oven 45 minutes, until tender. Remove from oven, peel and mash pulp with fork. Add salt, garlic, and lemon juice. Then add tahini, stirring rapidly to form a paste.[3] Place in shallow serving dish and let stand at room temperature until serving time, allowing at least ½ hour for flavor to develop. Pour oil over surface and sprinkle with cumin just before serving.

Tabouli is the name for a salad composed mainly of softened wheat, chopped parsley, and mint. The chopping and dicing are the time-consuming elements. The salad is served in scoops of lettuce leaves and packed into the pita bread along with the Fallafel.

TABOULI

Yield: 4 servings
Preparation time: 15 minutes

¼ cup cracked wheat
1 cup water
2 cups chopped parsley[4]
¼ cup chopped mint
½ cucumber, peeled and diced
1 tomato, diced

2 scallions, thinly sliced
3 tablespoons lemon juice
3 tablespoons oil
¼ teaspoon salt
Large lettuce leaves
Olives, optional

Soak wheat in water about 15 minutes. Drain well squeezing out moisture. Toss parsley, mint, cucumber, tomato, scallion, and soaked wheat together. Add lemon juice, oil, and salt, and mix to coat all ingredients. Serve immediately on lettuce-lined plate with garnish of olives or chill until needed.

[4] A kitchen scissors is ideal for chopping greens and cuts down on work.

Directions are given here for Homemade Tahini—a high-protein sesame seed paste. For convenience I would suggest buying ready-made tahini. It is found in Mideastern stores, specialty stores and many health food stores. If you can't locate any, make your own. The meal merits the time spent on it!

HOMEMADE TAHINI

Utensils: blender
Yield: 1 cup
Preparation time: 15 minutes
Oven temperature: 350° F.

1⅓ *cups sesame seeds*
⅓ *cup oil*
¼ *teaspoon salt*

Spread sesame seeds in shallow pan and toast in 350° F. oven 10 minutes. Blend seeds at high speed of blender until powdery. Add oil gradually at low speed, blending until smooth. Add salt. Store in covered container at room temperature.

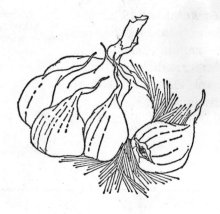

The Tahini Sauce is spooned over the Fallafel at serving time.

TAHINI SAUCE

Yield: about 1 cup; 4 servings
Preparation time: 5 minutes

½ cup tahini
1 clove garlic, crushed
1 teaspoon salt

¼ cup lemon juice
½ to ¾ cup water

Mix tahini with garlic and salt. Add lemon juice. Beat in ¼ cup water. Beat in remaining ¼ to ½ cup water, 1 tablespoon at a time, until sauce is of thick pouring consistency.

One of the most popular dishes from the Mideast, Fallafel has recently become popular in the United States. Fallafel stands are springing up in many parts of the country. Fallafel are small deep fried fritters made from puréed chick peas. They can be served on a plate with Tahini Sauce spooned over, or, more authentically, assembled in the following manner: Cut pita bread across the diameter and open pocket. Insert 2 to 4 fried chick pea balls, top with Tabouli, and spoon Tahini Sauce over all. You are now holding the Mideast equivalent of the hot dog.

FALLAFEL

Utensils: food mill; deep pot for frying; fat thermometer
Yield: 16 balls; 4 servings
Preparation time: 10 minutes
Cooking time: 15 to 20 minutes

3 cups cooked chick peas[5]
About ½ cup cooking liquid
2 teaspoons salt
2 teaspoons chopped parsley
2 cloves garlic, crushed
¼ teaspoon pepper

2 small or 1 large egg,
  lightly beaten
About ¼ cup whole wheat
  cracker crumbs
Oil for deep fat frying

Purée chick peas in food mill adding liquid as needed. Add remaining ingredients to purée. Shape into 16 balls about 1 inch in diameter[6]; flatten balls slightly. Chill until cooking time. Pour oil into deep pot until ⅓ full. Heat to 375° F. Fry Fallafel, 4 at a time, until brown and crisp on the outside, about 5 minutes. Drain well. Keep warm in low oven until serving time.[7]

[5] To prepare chick peas, soak about 1¼ cups dried chick peas overnight in 3 cups water or bring to boil 2 minutes, remove from heat and let stand 1 hour. Cook soaked peas over low heat, 1½ to 2 hours, until tender.

[6] If mixture is too soft to shape add additional crumbs.

[7] To reuse oil, cool and pour through strainer or cheesecloth back into bottle. Let rest a week to regain its strength before reusing. Use only for deep frying.

Menu #15

BORSCHT WITH SLICED CUCUMBER
BOILED KASHA PIROGEN
BLENDED COTTAGE CHEESE

Serving Suggestions: Russian cooking inspired this menu. These and similar foods are featured on the menu of dairy restaurants so if you live in a city that has a dairy restaurant, you can enjoy them out as well as in your own home.

Cooking Schedule: Borscht is usually served cold and must be made at least 3 hours before serving. Stores well in refrigerator for several weeks.

The pirogen take several different steps to prepare, but these can be done at the same time in about 30 minutes. They can be cooked as soon as they are made or held several hours. Begin the final cooking preparations about 30 minutes before dinner so the cooking water has a chance to boil.

The cottage cheese can be blended while the pirogen boil.

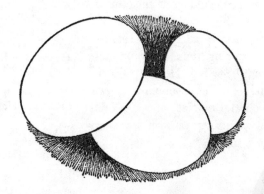

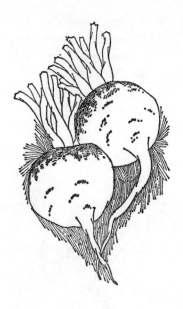

Borscht is a beet soup which when served cold is traditionally garnished with sliced egg, boiled potato, sour cream, fresh vegetables, or any combination of these. A first course or light main dish. It keeps several weeks under refrigeration.

BORSCHT WITH CUCUMBER

Utensils: large saucepan with cover
Yield: 5 to 6 cups; 4 to 6 servings
Preparation time: under 10 minutes
Cooking time: 35 minutes

4 medium beets (about 2 pounds)
1 cup chopped onion
1½ teaspoons salt

4 cups water
1½ tablespoons raw sugar
1 tablespoon lemon juice
Sliced cucumber rounds

[1] If not thoroughly chilled by serving time add 1 ice cube to each bowl.

Peel beets and chop to make 3½ to 4 cups. Combine beets, onion, salt, and water in saucepan. Bring to boil, cover, reduce heat and cook 35 minutes. Add sugar and lemon juice and chill thoroughly.[1] Float several slices of cucumber in each bowl to serve.

Cooked buckwheat groats, a delicious meal in itself with fried onions, boiled potatoes, and blended cottage cheese, is here cooked soft and used to fill homemade noodles. The finished dish features chewy noodle bundles with a creamy topping. Serve with plenty of salt to taste.

BOILED KASHA PIROGEN

Utensils: small saucepan with cover; small skillet; rolling pin; large kettle or stew pot
Yield: 8 pirogen; 2 servings[2]
Preparation time: 30 minutes
Cooking time: 15 to 20 minutes

¼ cup buckwheat groats (kasha)
½ teaspoon salt
¾ cup boiling water
1 tablespoon oil
1 onion, chopped

1 cup plus 1 tablespoon whole wheat flour
1 egg
1 tablespoon water
1 tablespoon oil
2 quarts boiling salted water

Place kasha and salt in small saucepan. Pour in boiling water, stir, cover, and cook over low heat until water is absorbed, 15 to 20 minutes.[3] Meanwhile chop onion and sauté in oil over medium heat about 10 minutes, until brown. Stir occasionally. While this cooking takes place prepare noodles. Combine flour, egg, water, and oil in bowl and mix with hands. Form into a ball and knead by squeezing between your fingers until smooth, about 5 minutes. Divide dough in half and roll each half on floured

[2] Use this recipe as a common denominator for as many servings as you need.

[3] Finished kasha will be mushy, unlike the fluffy version traditionally served alone.

board or oilcloth to form 2 thin sheets 8 inches square. Cut each into 8 rectangles 4×2 inches each. Mix cooked kasha and fried onion together thoroughly. Spread about 1½ tablespoons kasha filling over each of 8 rectangles. Top with remaining rectangles and pinch edges with moist fingers to seal. Any holes in the noodles can be patched with a thick paste of flour and water. Cook in boiling water 15 to 20 minutes until tender, but chewy. Do not handle roughly. Drain well and serve with Blended Cottage Cheese. To store several hours, place uncooked pirogen on a clean cloth, cover, and let stand at room temperature.

Blended Cottage Cheese is a high-protein substitute for sour cream (and low-calorie as well) and can replace sour cream in all recipes that don't require cooking.

BLENDED COTTAGE CHEESE

Place 1 cup (8 ounces) cottage cheese in blender container. Add 2 to 2½ tablespoons water or milk and purée until smooth. Add additional liquid if needed.

Menu #16

MACARONI SHELLS WITH VEGETABLE SAUCE
CHEESE WEDGES
KIDNEY BEAN SALAD

Serving Suggestions: A simple meal to prepare for any number by multiplying or dividing ingredients proportionately. Serve macaroni in shallow soup plates for easy eating.

Cooking Schedule: The salad calls for cooked beans which can be cooked up to a week in advance and stored in the refrigerator. If you like you can make the salad a day in advance or up to 10 minutes before serving. The longer it marinates, the more developed the flavor.

Cheese tastes best at room temperature so take it from the refrigerator when you begin preparing dinner.

Allow 30 to 35 minutes cooking time for sauce and 5 minutes to do any chopping of vegetables beforehand. While the sauce simmers cook the macaroni shells. They require 15 minutes cooking time in boiling water so begin about 10 minutes after sauce begins to cook. Sauce can be held and reheated if necessary.

A protein rich salad which is equally good made with kidney beans, chick peas, or white beans—whatever you have on hand.

KIDNEY BEAN SALAD

Yield: 4 servings
Preparation time: under 5 minutes

2 cups cooked kidney beans
6 scallions, chopped
1 teaspoon salt
3 tablespoons vinegar

2 tablespoons oil
¼ teaspoon ground
coriander, optional

Toss all ingredients in bowl. Marinate at room temperature up to 30 minutes, or in refrigerator if being held longer.

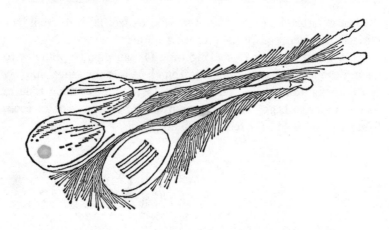

The rich tomato sauce here is made in minutes. Shorten cooking time if you like your vegetables crisp. Macaroni shells made with whole wheat flour and Jerusalem artichoke pulp are available at most health food outlets.

VEGETABLE SAUCE

Utensils: large skillet
Yield: 4 servings
Preparation time: 5 minutes
Cooking time: 30 to 35 minutes

2 tablespoons oil
1 large clove garlic, minced
1 large or 2 small onions, chopped
1 green pepper, cut in thin strips
6 tomatoes, diced
3 medium zucchini, coarsely chopped

1½ teaspoons salt
1 teaspoon dried basil
1 teaspoon dried oregano
½ teaspoon dried rosemary
¼ teaspoon pepper sauce
20 small whole mushrooms

Heat oil in skillet. Sauté garlic over medium heat 1 minute. Add chopped onion and continue to cook until tender. Add green pepper, tomato, zucchini, and salt. Cook over low heat until soft, about 10 minutes. Add basil, oregano, rosemary, and pepper sauce and cook until thickened, another 10 minutes. Add mushrooms and simmer 10 to 15 minutes longer. Spoon over cooked macaroni shells in serving plate.

MACARONI SHELLS

Yield: 4 servings
Cooking time: 20 minutes

   1 *quart water*
   ½ *teaspoon salt*
   3 *cups, about ¾ pound, small macaroni shells*

Bring salted water to boil in large pot. Add shells, return to boil, and cook in boiling water 10 to 15 minutes, until just tender. Drain and rinse with cold water to stop cooking. Return to pot and cover until needed.

CHEESE WEDGES

Allow 1 to 2 ounces favorite cheese per person. Brie, Camembert, Swiss, or Cheddar are widely available and all go well if you want a safe bet; or, experiment with other natural cheeses on the market.

Menu ✳17

VEGETABLE-CHEESE CURRY
FILLED BREADS
ONION-CARROT SALAD

Serving Suggestions: All the dishes are taken from Indian favorites and are mild to suit unaccustomed palates. If you like these, go through some Indian cookbooks for additional recipes. Many Indians are vegetarians and a variety of their traditional foods can be adapted to your tastes. The recipes here can be easily divided in half for two or multiplied for additional servings.

Cooking Schedule: Begin 40 minutes before dinner with the bread, allowing about 15 minutes to prepare and assemble. The final cooking can be done while the curry cooks.

Allow 25 minutes for the Vegetable-Cheese Curry from start to finish. The first 5 to 10 are for preparation; the last 10 to 15 for cooking.

While the curry cooks fry the breads. They don't require much attention so you can put the salad together at the same time. If you prefer, the salad can be made first. This will give you a little time to relax before dinner. You'll need about 10 minutes to prepare the salad.

These breads take on the flavor of the filling which you can vary to your taste. They are crisp, tasty, and easier than you'd expect to fix.

FILLED BREADS

Utensils: rolling pin; large skillet or griddle
Yield: 8 3-inch breads
Preparation time: 15 minutes; varies with skill
Cooking time: about 10 minutes

1 cup whole wheat flour   *¼ cup cooked peas[1]*
½ teaspoon salt   *2 carrots, grated*
4 teaspoons oil
2 to 3 tablespoons warm
* water*

[1] Other vegetables of your choice, cooked or finely chopped, can replace those suggested. Try cooked sweet potato, radish, turnip, cauliflower.

[2] I find rolling dough between two sheets of waxed or oiled paper prevents sticking and avoids use of additional flour.

Mix flour and salt. Blend in oil and enough water to allow dough to be kneaded without crumbling. Form dough into a ball and knead briefly to form a smooth dough. Divide dough into 16 small balls. Flatten each ball lightly with palm of hand, then roll out to form a very thin pancake.[2] Turn dough when necessary to keep pancake round and flat on both sides. Mash cooked peas with back of spoon or fork. Spread mashed peas in center of four of the pancakes. Cover with an unfilled round and pinch edges together to seal with slightly moistened fingers. Place grated carrot on four remaining pancakes and top with four unfilled rounds; seal. Fry immediately or cover with a slightly damp cloth and set aside until ready. To fry, heat large skillet over medium flame. Wipe surface with oiled paper towel to grease lightly. Fry breads until crisp and lightly browned on each side. Push back and forth occasionally with fingers to keep them from sticking. Keep fried breads warm in oven while others cook. Serve warm, 2 per person, one with each filling.

A mild curry with a distinctive, but not hot, flavor. Best served in a flat bowl to preserve the tasty sauce. In traditional Indian fashion the list of spices is long, but don't let that throw you—the preparation is simple.

VEGETABLE-CHEESE CURRY

Utensils: large saucepan with cover
Yield: 4 servings
Preparation time: 5 to 10 minutes
Cooking time: 10 to 15 minutes

3 tablespoons oil
½ pound farmer cheese, cut in ½ inch cubes
4 cloves
4 teaspoons cinnamon
¼ teaspoon ground cardamom
¼ teaspoon crushed red pepper or pepper sauce
2½ teaspoons ground ginger
2 teaspoons turmeric
½ teaspoon chili powder
1 teaspoon ground cumin
2 tomatoes, cubed
1 cauliflower, cut in flowerets
1½ teaspoons salt
1 teaspoon raw sugar
1 cup water
1 lemon, cut in wedges

Heat oil in saucepan. Add cheese; fry 2 to 3 minutes over low heat, being careful not to break cheese. Remove from pan to plate and reserve. Add cloves, cinnamon, cardamom, and pepper to pot and fry 1 minute. Add ginger, turmeric, chili powder, and cumin and fry 1 to 2 minutes. Add tomato, cauliflowerets, salt, sugar, water; cover and cook until cauliflower is tender, about 10 minutes. To serve, place ¼ cheese cubes in each bowl, spoon vegetable mixture over cheese, and garnish with lemon wedge. Let each person squeeze in lemon juice to taste.

A piquant salad, very unusual and refreshing. The limes add the bite.

ONION-CARROT SALAD

Yield: 4 servings
Preparation time: 10 minutes

1 teaspoon salt
½ teaspoon ground turmeric
½ teaspoon dry mustard
¼ teaspoon chili powder
1 teaspoon raw sugar

1 large onion, thinly sliced
1 cup shredded carrots
2 limes, unpeeled, thinly sliced

Mix spices together. Place onion, carrot, and lime slices in salad bowl, add mixed spices and toss.

Menu #18

MOM'S THICK SPLIT PEA SOUP
MILL VALLEY SANDWICHES
CRUNCHY PICKLES

Serving Suggestions: A filling meal, especially welcome in cold weather. For warmer days, choose a lighter soup.

Cooking Schedule: Prepare pickles at least 6 hours in advance. They can be stored in refrigerator several weeks.

Begin soup 1½ hours before serving time. Soup can be reheated as necessary and refrigerated several days if you wish. Soup that is reheated is thicker than when just made.

Prepare sandwiches just before dinner.

Homemade cucumber pickles that are delicate and sweet. They lose their crunchiness as they stand, but are just as tasty.

CRUNCHY PICKLES

Yield: 12 pickles
Preparation time: 5 minutes
Waiting time: 6 hours

2 unwaxed cucumbers[1]
½ onion
1 small clove garlic, crushed
1 tablespoon fresh or 2 teaspoons dried dill

1 cup water
3 tablespoons cider vinegar
2 tablespoons raw sugar
1 tablespoon salt

Wash cucumbers and slice each lengthwise into six slices. Spread in shallow container in layers. Slice onion into rings and place over cucumbers. Sprinkle garlic and dill on top. Mix water, vinegar, sugar, and salt. Pour over cucumbers to cover. Cover and refrigerate at least 6 hours. To store, place pickles, onions, and brine in tightly covered jar. Brine can be reused—add a tablespoon vinegar and 2 teaspoons raw sugar to remaining brine and pour over new batch of sliced cucumber and onion.

[1] If unwaxed cucumbers cannot be found use waxed cucumbers and peel them.

Split Pea Soup is a nourishing potage that is thick and rich and very warming.

MOM'S THICK SPLIT PEA SOUP

Utensils: large pot with cover
Yield: 4 servings[2]
Preparation time: 5 minutes
Cooking time: 1½ hours

1 *cup dried green split peas*	3 *celery tops*
	1 *bay leaf*
4 *cups water*	2 *teaspoons salt*
1 *onion, chopped*	¼ *teaspoon pepper*
2 *carrots, pared and chopped*	

[2] For additional servings use equal proportions of all ingredients.

[3] While water comes to boil remaining ingredients can be prepared.

Wash peas well with cold water and drain. Place in large saucepan, add water and bring to boil.[3] Add remaining ingredients, reduce heat to the lowest point, cover, and cook 1½ hours. Remove cover

and mash with fork or in food mill. Cook
without cover several minutes to thicken
if necessary. Adjust seasoning to taste.
For a thinner soup, purée in blender.
Serve very hot.

These tasty cheese sandwiches were inspired by a version we had
out in California. A unique taste worth repeating. Try it on a
variety of breads.

MILL VALLEY SANDWICHES

For each person spread a slice of whole wheat bread with homemade or safflower oil mayonnaise. Place several spinach leaves on
top. Cover with a layer of natural munster cheese, spread alfalfa
or bean sprouts over cheese, and finish sandwich with another
slice of whole wheat bread, spread with mayonnaise if you like.

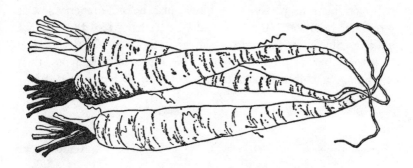

Menu #19

Serving Suggestions: An excellent choice for entertaining because it can be prepared in advance. And, because final cooking is brief, you can do this last-minute work after guests have arrived and neither the food nor the company will have to wait.

Cooking Schedule: There are a number of alternatives here, your choice governed by your own time schedule. The batter for the crepes takes 2 minutes to prepare, but should stand at least 1 hour before cooking. The batter can remain in the refrigerator several hours if necessary without harm. The crepes themselves take about 20 busy minutes to make. If you like you can make them in advance and refrigerate up to 2 days or freeze for 2 to 3 weeks.

Allow 20 minutes to prepare the filling. It can be made up to 1 day in advance and held in the refrigerator until needed.

The entire dish can be assembled and refrigerated several hours if this is best.

If you plan to prepare everything just before dinner allow 1 busy hour from start (that's after the batter has rested the required hour) to finish. In this case, begin with the rice—almost no time to prepare but 45 minutes to cook. Next prepare the crepes, then the filling, assemble all and then toss the salad together.

A kitchen staple, brown rice, tossed with nuts and raisins, made aromatic with a sprinkling of cinnamon, becomes delicate and festive.

NUTTED RICE WITH RAISINS

Utensils: saucepan with tight fitting lid
Yield: 4 servings
Preparation time: 5 minutes
Cooking time: 45 minutes

1¼ cups raw brown rice[1]
2½ cups water
¼ cup raisins
¼ cup sliced almonds
2 tablespoons pine nuts
¼ teaspoon cinnamon

Wash rice well in cold water and drain completely. Place in saucepan, add water, and bring to boil. Cover, turn heat very low, and cook slowly 40 to 45 minutes, until liquid is completely absorbed. Do not stir during cooking time. When cooked, remove cover partially to allow steam to escape. Add raisins, almonds, pine nuts, sprinkle with cinnamon, toss with a fork, and replace cover until needed.

[1] Servings here are based on side dish portions, as this is a filling meal. If at any time you would like larger servings add more rice and use twice as much water as rice.

Crepes are thin pancakes which are loved by all, surprisingly easy to make, but time-consuming since they are made one by one, each taking about a minute. They can be filled with any vegetable combination as a main dish, or with fruit or fruit purée, jam, or cream as dessert. The filling here is a combination of mushrooms and spinach with provolone adding a cheesy flavor. Walnuts, which are optional, are included for an interesting crunchiness.

CREPES

Utensils: blender or beater; small (6- to 8-inch) frying pan with sloped sides
Yield: about 16 crepes
Preparation time: 5 minutes
Resting time: 1 hour
Cooking time: 20 minutes

½ cup milk
½ cup water
2 eggs
1 cup whole wheat flour

2 tablespoons oil or melted butter
1 teaspoon salt

2 Pan is greased lightly before the first crepe only.

Combine all ingredients in blender container or mixing bowl. Blend at medium speed or beat until smooth. Refrigerate at least 1 hour. Batter should be consistency of heavy cream when you begin cooking. It thickens on standing. If too thick add more milk. To cook, place pan on medium heat and allow to get fairly hot. Dampen a paper towel with oil and wipe surface of heated pan.[2] Make crepe by pouring about 3 tablespoons batter into center of pan, holding pan by the handle as you add the batter. Quickly tilt the pan in all directions so batter forms a thin coating over the surface. Pour any batter that does not stick back into uncooked batter. Place pan over medium heat and cook until edges pull away from sides of pan. Lift crepe and turn to cook other side briefly.[3] I find my fingers best for turning the crepe. Transfer crepe, pale side up, to plate or waxed paper and continue until all batter is used.[4] Do not pile cooked crepes directly on top of each other; place side by side or with waxed paper in between. Each crepe will take from 1 to 2 minutes. The heat of the pan and your familiarity with the procedure are the key factors and as you progress cooking time decreases. Your goal is a tender, thin pancake, delicately browned on one side. Use crepes immediately or wrap with paper between and store in refrigerator or freezer. Allow frozen crepes to thaw before separating.

[3] The second side will not brown and need only cook about 30 seconds.

[4] Don't worry if the first crepe sticks—your pan probably wasn't hot enough. There's plenty of batter for a few mistakes so simply wipe any cooked batter off the pan and go on.

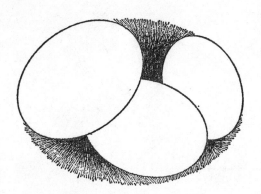

SPINACH FILLING

Utensils: large skillet
Yield: filling for 16 to 20 crepes
Preparation time (including cooking): 20 minutes

1 tablespoon oil or butter
½ pound mushrooms, chopped

2 cups chopped raw spinach
½ cup chopped walnuts, optional

Heat oil in skillet. Add mushrooms and cook, stirring occasionally, until tender, about 10 minutes. Add spinach, cover and cook 5 minutes, until wilted. Remove from heat and add walnuts.

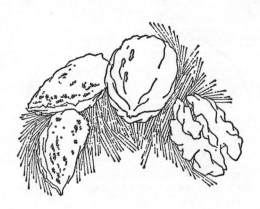

SPINACH CREPES

Utensils: shallow casserole or baking dish
Yield: 4 servings[5]
Preparation time: 5 minutes
Baking time: 10 minutes[6]
Oven temperature: 350° F.

Crepes (above)
Spinach Filling (above)
20 thin slices provolone
   cheese

Oil
Paste of 1 teaspoon potato
   starch mixed with 1
   tablespoon water, optional

Place 1 slice provolone to cover the pale side of each crepe. Drain filling, reserving liquid if desired. Place 1 tablespoon filling on each crepe and roll. Lightly grease baking dish to keep crepes from sticking. Place rolled crepes, seam side down, directly next to one another in baking dish. More than one layer of crepes can be made if necessary. Tear any remaining cheese into small pieces and place over crepes. Spoon any remaining filling on top. If desired, potato starch paste can be stirred into remaining liquid, cooked until thickened, and spooned on top with remaining filling to form a sauce. Place baking dish in 350° F. oven and bake 10 minutes, until cheese melts. Serve hot.

[5] This yield is based on hearty appetites and can serve up to six depending on who the six are.

[6] Crepes can be assembled and refrigerated several hours until needed. In this case allow 15 minutes baking time.

Endive is an often neglected vegetable. Its mild, pleasant, slightly bitter flavor and crisp texture are a nice variation in salad greens.

TOMATO ENDIVE SALAD

Yield: 4 servings
Preparation time: 5 minutes

2 endives, cut in half
   lengthwise
2 tomatoes, sliced
1½ tablespoons wine vinegar

½ tablespoon lemon juice
3 tablespoons oil
½ clove garlic, crushed
Salt and pepper

Combine vinegar, lemon juice, oil, and garlic in salad bowl. Cut each tomato slice in quarters. Place endive and tomato in salad bowl and toss to cover with dressing. Sprinkle with salt and a few grindings of pepper to taste.

APPLE JUICE

Choose unsweetened apple juice with no preservatives and serve throughout the meal as desired.

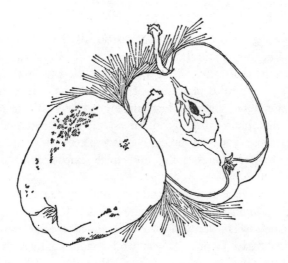

Menu #20

Serving Suggestions: If you want to do all the work yourself, go ahead. But, for a meal that's fun for all, serve the Vegetable Tempura fondue style, letting everyone cook their own vegetables at the table. A word of warning though—if you're in a rush to go out better serve the tempura already cooked. It's a long meal around the chafing dish—good for an evening's entertainment. As a compromise you can prepare a few pieces of tempura in the kitchen to get things going and quell impatient appetites.

Cooking Schedule: If you're going to use homemade noodles allow yourself 30 to 45 minutes to prepare the dough. They can, however, be prepared whenever you like and stored several months in a tightly covered container as you would store commercial varieties.

Once the noodles are made follow either of the cooking schedules given below:

If you plan to cook the meal in the kitchen: Prepare the vegetables for the tempura first, either 40 minutes before dinner or ahead of time, keeping them well chilled until cooking time. Prepare the salad. Now put the water up to boil for the noodles, heat the oil for the tempura, assemble all ingredients for the broth, and then prepare the tempura batter. As you deep-fry the vegetables prepare the soup and the noodles. Keep the cooked vegetables warm in the oven. The total time for these three operations is under 30 minutes.

If you're going to let everyone cook his own tempura at the table: Prepare the vegetables for cooking and chill. Fifteen minutes before dinner cook the noodles and the broth. While they cook prepare the salad, heat the oil in a fondue pot or chafing dish and mix up the tempura batter. Then, set the fondue pot over a sterno or alcohol burner at the table, arrange the prepared vegetables on each plate, put the dish of batter on the table, and let everyone cook their own, holding the batter coated vegetables on a fondue fork. They can enjoy the Noodles in Broth and salad as the vegetables cook.

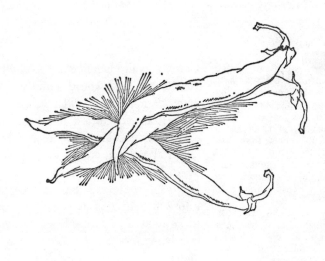

Buckwheat and whole wheat noodles are available in health food stores. If you'd like to have some fun though, try your hand at the homemade kind. Both are cooked the same way as commercial varieties. The resulting dish, however, has more flavor and texture.

HOMEMADE WHOLE WHEAT NOODLES

Utensils: clean hands; rolling pin[1]
Yield: about 2 pounds; enough for 8 to 12 servings
Preparation time: 30 to 45 minutes

> 4 cups whole wheat flour   1 teaspoon salt
> 4 eggs   5 tablespoons water

Combine all ingredients, blend with your hands and knead until very stiff, about 5 minutes. Divide dough into 4 balls. Roll each into a rectangle, rolling as thin as possible.[2] Roll each rectangle jelly roll fashion, cut to desired width— ¼ to ½ inch is a nice size—and spread to dry.[3] Noodles can be left long or cut into 2-inch lengths as you like. Noodles to be used at once need not go through the drying process. When dry, store noodles in covered container. To cook noodles: For 4 servings, bring 2 quarts water to boil; add 3 cups (about ¾ pound) store-bought or homemade noodles. Return to boil and cook 10 to 15 minutes, until tender but not soft. Drain and rinse quickly with cold water.[4]

[1] If you are particularly fond of homemade pasta a pasta machine is a worthwhile investment. This small hand-cranked machine enables you to roll and cut pasta like a pro. Cost ranges from $10 to $25. Prepare dough as directed here, then follow manufacturer's instructions for rolling and cutting the pasta.

[2] It is sometimes easier to roll dough after it has been allowed to rest about 10 minutes. I would suggest partially rolling each ball, going on to the next ones, and going back to each rectangle to get it rolled really thin.

[3] Allow noodles to dry in the open air several hours or overnight. They should be stiff, but not crumbly.

[4] Noodles can be reheated if need be. Just pour boiling water over cooked noodles and drain.

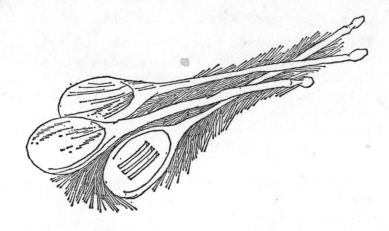

The noodles are served in a bowl of salty broth. Try eating them with chopsticks, then drink the broth.

TAMARI BROTH

Utensils: covered saucepan
Yield: 4 servings
Preparation time: 5 minutes
Cooking time: 10 minutes

8 scallions, minced
1 tablespoon oil
4 cups water

1 teaspoon salt
¼ cup Tamari or pure soy sauce

Sauté scallions in oil in saucepan about 1 minute. Add water, bring to boil, cover, reduce heat, and simmer about 10 minutes. Add salt and soy sauce, bring to boil again and pour over noodles in individual serving bowls.

The vegetables are deep fried in batter to bring forth piping hot vegetables in a crunchy coating. The trick is to have the vegetables well chilled and the batter fresh. Cooked pieces can be kept warm in a low oven, but they will loose their crispness after a while.

VEGETABLE TEMPURA

Utensils: frying thermometer; deep pot for frying or fondue pot and warmer
Yield: 4 servings
Preparation time: 10 to 15 minutes
Cooking time: about 3 minutes per vegetable when done at the table. About 30 minutes in the kitchen
Frying temperature: 350° F.

> *Prepared vegetables*[5]
> ½ *cup whole wheat flour*
> ½ *cup corn flour or finely ground corn meal*
> ½ *teaspoon salt*
> 1 *egg, lightly beaten*
> 1 *cup water*
> *Oil for deep frying*

[5] For each person prepare— 2 cauliflowerets, 2 small stalks broccoli, 2 small spears asparagus, 2 whole mushrooms, 3 slices carrot cut on a diagonal, 2 slices parsnip cut on a diagonal, 1 whole green bean, 1 slice sweet potato—or any combination of the above allowing 10 to 15 pieces per serving. You can try other vegetables; just keep the pieces a manageable size. Celery and green pepper taste great but it is difficult to get the batter to adhere to them.

Pour oil to reach ⅓ the depth of the pot to be used for deep-fat frying and heat to 350° F. Meanwhile, mix together flours, salt, egg, and water until thoroughly moistened. Don't worry about lumps. Dip cold vegetable into batter. Let excess batter drop back into bowl. Cook coated vegetables, 4 or 5 at a time, in hot oil until browned. Drain on absorbent paper. Place in low oven to keep warm until needed. For individual cooking, allow vegetable to cool a bit before you take a bite . . . its hot inside!

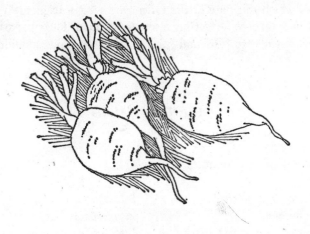

GINGER SAUCE

The individual pieces of Vegetable Tempura can be dunked into plain Tamari Soy Sauce or a Ginger Sauce made by grating peeled fresh ginger to taste into the Tamari Soy Sauce.

Salads which originate in the Orient are a bit foreign to Western palates and take some getting used to at first. They make lovely accompaniments to Oriental meals, however, and shouldn't be ignored.

ORIENTAL SALAD

Yield: 4 servings
Preparation time: 5 minutes

1 *large or 2 small bunches watercress*	1 *teaspoon soy sauce*
8 *fresh water chestnuts*	½ *teaspoon salt*
2 *teaspoons peanut or sesame seed oil*	1 *teaspoon raw sugar*

Wash watercress well, pat dry and cut off tough stems. Chop leaves and remaining stems with sharp knife or cleaver. Peel water chestnuts, wash in cold water, and chop. Combine the remaining ingredients in bowl, add the chopped vegetables, and stir well to coat. Refrigerate until serving time.

Menu #21

LENTILBURGERS WITH CHOPPED TOMATO SAUCE
HERBED YELLOW SQUASH
DAVID'S FRESH GREEN PEAS

Cooking Schedule: Begin a little over an hour before dinner so lentils have a chance to cook. You can do the rest of the preparation of the burgers while the lentils are cooking. Prepare ingredients for the sauce during this time as well. If desired, mixture can be prepared early in the day and refrigerated until cooking time. Final cooking should begin 20 minutes before dinner. Prepare squash while burgers and sauce cook.

Lentilburgers are high-protein patties with a hint of sweetness. Four make a hearty main dish for anyone. The entire recipe makes 8 servings. If you're serving fewer people freeze the leftovers.

LENTILBURGERS

Utensils: large saucepan with cover; blender or food mill; large skillet or baking sheet
Yield: 8 servings
Preparation time: 10 minutes
Cooking time: 1 hour and 5 minutes
Oven temperature (optional): 350° F.

1½ cups dried lentils	2 bay leaves
4 cups water	1 carrot, cut in pieces
1 small onion	2 teaspoons salt

Rinse lentils in cold water and drain. Place in large saucepan. Add remaining ingredients, bring to boil, cover, reduce heat, and cook 45 minutes. Drain, reserving ½ cup cooking liquid.[1] Discard onion and bay leaves. Purée cooked lentils, carrot, and reserved liquid at high speed in blender or in food mill until smooth.

Puréed lentils	2 eggs, beaten
1 medium onion, chopped	½ cup corn meal
1 clove garlic, minced	½ cup wheat germ
1 rib celery with tops, chopped	6 tablespoons molasses
3 tablespoons chopped parsley	2 tablespoons vinegar
	1½ teaspoons dry mustard

[1] Any additional liquid from cooked lentils should be used for soup.

Combine all ingredients. *To fry*: lightly grease skillet and heat. Spoon mixture onto hot skillet, allowing ¼ cup per burger. Cook until brown, about 10 minutes, turn and brown other side. Keep fried burgers warm in oven while remaining burgers are cooking. *To bake*: spoon mixture into mounds of ¼ cup each onto well-greased baking sheet. Bake in 350° F. oven 20 minutes.[2] Extra lentilburgers can be cooked, wrapped individually for freezing, placed together in a heavy plastic bag, and frozen successfully up to 3 months.

[2] For crisp burgers, fry. Baked burgers are moister, but do not have the crunchy outside.

Here's a quick tomato sauce with texture and a mildly sweet taste. Spoon it over the Lentilburgers at serving time.

CHOPPED TOMATO SAUCE

Preparation time: 5 minutes
Cooking time: 20 minutes

2 tablespoons oil
2 onions, chopped
1 green pepper, chopped
6 medium tomatoes,
   chopped

1½ teaspoons salt
1 tablespoon molasses

Heat oil in saucepan. Add onion and green pepper and cook until tender but not brown. Add tomatoes, salt and molasses and cook over medium heat 15 minutes.

DAVID'S FRESH GREEN PEAS

Serve raw peas in the pod and let everyone shell their own at the table. Allow 2 pounds for 4 servings.

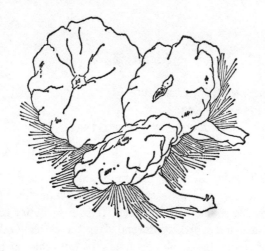

Yellow summer squash is a mild-flavored vegetable, perked up by the addition of herbs.

HERBED SQUASH

Utensils: small saucepan or skillet with cover
Yield: 4 servings
Preparation time: under 5 minutes
Cooking time: 5 to 10 minutes

2 *large or 4 small yellow squash*	2 *sprigs dill*
¼ *cup water*	½ *teaspoon dried rosemary*
2 *sprigs parsley*	½ *teaspoon salt*

Slice squash into rounds. Do not peel. Combine water, herbs, and salt. Bring to a boil. Add squash, reduce heat, cover, and steam 5 to 10 minutes, until crisp-tender.

Menu ※22

CHEESE AND VEGETABLE PIE
PAN-FRIED CABBAGE
WALNUT BREAD WITH APPLE BUTTER

Cooking Schedule: Because the bread should stand 20 minutes before baking and cool at least 20 minutes before slicing it should be prepared 1½ hours before dinner. It is even better made a day ahead of time and will keep several days thereafter. Only about 5 minutes of your time are required to put this loaf together.

Start the Cheese and Vegetable Pie 45 minutes before dinner, giving you 10 minutes to prepare the vegetables and assemble the pie before the 35-minute baking period.

Prepare cabbage while pie bakes.

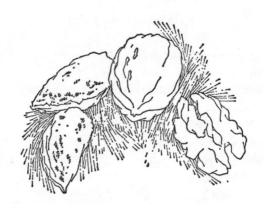

A sweet quick bread is the final product here, small in volume but moist and flavorful. Use leftovers for tea-type sandwiches.

WALNUT BREAD

Utensils: 8×4×2-inch loaf pan
Yield: 1 loaf
Preparation time: 5 minutes
Baking time: 45 minutes
Oven temperature: 350° F.

1½ cups whole wheat flour
¼ teaspoon salt
2 teaspoons baking powder
½ cup honey
¼ cup oil

2 eggs
½ cup apple juice
½ cup coarsely chopped
   walnuts

Mix together dry ingredients. Make a well in center and add honey, oil, eggs, and juice. Stir until all ingredients are moistened and evenly blended. Stir in nuts. Pour into well greased 8×4×2-inch loaf pan and let stand 20 minutes.[1] Bake in 350° F. oven until delicately browned, 45 minutes. Cool in pan 10 minutes, then turn onto a wire rack and cool before slicing.

[1] A 20-minute resting period improves the texture of baking powder breads.

Cheese and chopped vegetables baked in a pie plate without a crust—the result is light, flavorful, and very satisfying.

CHEESE AND VEGETABLE PIE

Utensils: beater; 9-inch pie plate
Yield: 4 servings
Preparation time: 10 minutes
Baking time: 35 minutes
Oven temperature: 350° F.

2 cups (1 pound) ricotta or farmer cheese[2]
2 eggs, separated
½ teaspoon salt
1 small carrot, chopped
1 small rib celery, chopped
3 tablespoons chopped green pepper
1 scallion, thinly sliced
3 small mushrooms, chopped

[2] Ricotta gives a creamier texture but either one is delicious.

[3] Small quantities of any other leftover vegetable odds and ends can be added as well.

[4] Stir 1 tablespoon or so of the beaten egg whites in initially to loosen the cheese, making folding in easier.

Combine cheese and egg yolks and beat together until smooth. Add seasonings and chopped vegetables[3] and mix well. Beat egg whites until stiff peaks form; fold into cheese-vegetable mixture.[4] Turn into a 9-inch pie plate and bake in 350° F. oven 35 minutes, until browned on top. Let pie cool 5 minutes, cut into 4 wedges and serve.

PAN-FRIED CABBAGE

Heat 2 tablespoons oil or butter in skillet, add 3 tablespoons sesame seeds and toast lightly 1 minute. Add 1 small head cabbage which has been cut into strips or coarsely shredded, stir to coat with fat and seeds, cover and steam over medium heat until wilted, about 10 minutes. Stir again just before serving. Enough for 4 to 6 people.

APPLE BUTTER

Pure, unsweetened apple butter is sold in health food stores, specialty shops, and many delicatessens and groceries. It is a rich sweet spread to be used on breads and crackers. Essentially, it is applesauce that has been cooked down to a thick purée.

Menu #23

Serving Suggestions: A fondue is the perfect way to let everyone participate in the meal. Each person spears his food on a long-handled fork into a common chafing dish which is set over a sterno or alcohol burner or a food warmer. If you don't have a fondue set it is easy enough to improvise with a saucepan as the chafing dish rigged up on a base with a candle or sterno set underneath as the warmer.

Cooking Schedule: Everything for this meal can be done in advance, leaving you only 5 minutes or so of preparation between the first course, the Gazpacho, and the main course.

Begin with the Gazpacho, to be prepared at least 4 hours ahead, preferably 1 to 2 days. The spiciness takes hold as it stands and it should be served icy cold.

The ingredients for the fondue can be measured and set aside at any time. This takes only a few minutes. The Bread Chunks can be cut (all the better if they're on the dry side at serving time) and the Tomatoes and Cauliflowerets can be washed and kept covered in the refrigerator.

The salad greens can be torn, coated with the lemon, and stored covered in a crisper or plastic bag in the refrigerator until serving time.

All these steps can be done several hours before dinner or in the half-hour preceding the meal.

Five minutes before dinner chop the garnish for the Gazpacho, remove the fondue ingredients from the refrigerator and rub the pot with the cut garlic. Now enjoy your soup.

After you've eaten the Gazpacho, assemble the fondue—it only takes about 5 minutes—and enjoy the rest of your meal.

Gazpacho is a cold Spanish soup with the taste of highly spiced tomatoes. It should be served as cold as possible and is very refreshing, especially in warm weather. It can be kept several days in the refrigerator.

GAZPACHO

Utensils: blender
Yield: 4½ cups; 4 servings
Preparation time: 5 minutes
Marinating time: 30 minutes

3-inch piece whole grain or pumpernickel bread	3 tablespoons oil
2½ cups cold water	3 tablespoons wine vinegar
1 small clove garlic, minced	4 tomatoes, cut into wedges
1 teaspoon salt	2 tablespoons minced onion
	¼ teaspoon pepper sauce

Remove crust from bread, tear soft inside into small pieces and moisten with ½ cup cold water. Add garlic, salt, oil, vinegar, tomatoes, onion, and pepper sauce; marinate at room temperature 30 minutes. Blend mixture at high speed of blender until tomato has been completely puréed. Blend in up to 2 cups cold water, just enough to make a thick soup. Chill. If soup is not cold enough at serving time place an ice cube in each bowl. Garnish each serving with chopped cucumber and chopped green pepper.

The classic Cheese Fondue takes on a new twist with apple juice instead of wine. The texture is still as rich and creamy as ever though and clings beautifully to the chunks of whole grain bread, cherry tomatoes and cauliflowerets which are suggested here to carry the cheesy sauce from chafing dish to mouth. If it's your first fondue, here's how it goes: each person receives a long fork, an assortment of vegetables, and bread chunks and is seated within arm's length of the common chafing dish. The vegetable or bread chunk is speared onto the fork, then dipped into the hot cheese mixture in the chafing dish, then eaten right from the fork (with care, it's hot), or transferred to a plate and eaten with a dinner fork.

CHEESE FONDUE

Utensils: chafing dish or saucepan[1]; warmer; long forks
Yield: directions given here for each serving
Preparation time: 5 minutes
Cooking time: 5 minutes

1 cup (¼ pound) grated Emmenthaler (Switzerland Swiss cheese)	½ cup apple juice
	1½ teaspoons lemon juice
	Pepper, nutmeg
1 teaspoon whole wheat flour	Bread chunks,[2] cauliflowerets,
Garlic	cherry tomatoes

[1] Choose an earthenware or heavy metal pot. Do not use one which is Teflon-coated. The cheese must cling to sides of pot to achieve the proper texture.

[2] If possible have a piece of crust on each Bread Chunk. Spear bread through soft side into crust to dip. Bread Chunks should be dry, so use

Combine grated cheese and flour. Rub chafing dish with cut clove of garlic, pour in apple juice and set over moderate heat. When apple juice just reaches boiling point add cheese by handfuls, stirring constantly after each addition until cheese is melted. When all the cheese is added bring the fondue to bubble briefly, then add the lemon juice and a sprinkling of pepper and nutmeg. Place in center of table over sterno or alcohol burner or food warmer. Let each person spear Bread Chunks, pieces of cauliflower and cherry tomatoes as they like and dunk into the Fondue.

old bread or cut chunks ahead of time to dry out (or dry in low oven). Cube old bread and store in freezer for your next fondue. Allow 20 minutes to thaw.

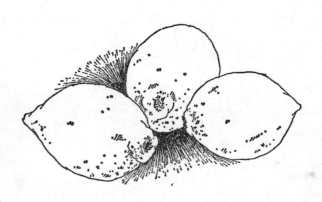

LEMON GREENS

Tear assorted salad greens—lettuce, escarole, spinach, Chinese cabbage or bok choy, watercress—into bite-size pieces. Squeeze lemon juice over greens and toss to coat well. Serve in salad bowls and let each person add oil and additional lemon or vinegar if desired, to taste.

Menu #24

IRISH STEW WITH PARSLEY DUMPLINGS
CREAMY FRUIT SALAD

Cooking Schedule: Begin 35 minutes before dinner. The stew comes first and the dumplings and salad can be made (in that order) in the 20 minutes needed for the stew to simmer. You'll need a large pot of boiling water for the dumplings, which can be started along with the stew so you'll have it good and hot when you're ready.

A vegetable stew is a real country dish with all the traditional Irish produce—cabbage, potatoes, leeks, turnips. This is the tastiest one I've had. Serve it in shallow bowls with Parsley Dumplings on top.

IRISH STEW

Utensils: large saucepan with cover
Yield: 4 servings
Preparation time: 15 minutes[1]
Cooking time: 30 minutes

3 tablespoons butter[2]
2 carrots, peeled
2 small white turnips, peeled
2 onions
2 leeks (well washed to
  remove sand)
1 small cabbage (about 1½
  pounds)

2 large potatoes, peeled
1 large tomato
1½ cups water
1 tablespoon salt
1 bay leaf

Melt butter in large saucepan. Cut carrots and turnips into ¼-inch slices. Add to melted butter, cover, and cook over low heat 5 minutes. Meanwhile, slice onion crosswise into rings, leeks across into 1-inch pieces, and quarter cabbage. Add to pot, cover, and cook 5 minutes. Cut potato into ¼-inch slices and quarter tomato. Add to pot with water, salt, and bay leaf. Cover and cook over medium heat 20 minutes, until vegetables are tender.

[1] Preparation can be done simultaneously with cooking.

[2] Butter adds to the flavor of the stew. Oil can be substituted if preferred.

These dumplings are light around the edges and chewy in the center—which is how we like them. For a lighter dumpling cover the pot while cooking and don't peek. They're not much to look at, but in a stew they're superb.

PARSLEY DUMPLINGS

Utensils: large stewing pot or Dutch oven
Yield: 12 dumplings; 4 servings
Preparation time: under 5 minutes
Cooking time: 15 minutes

2 quarts boiling water	2 eggs, lightly beaten
1½ cups whole wheat flour	1½ teaspoons salt
½ cup water	¼ cup chopped parsley

Have water boiling in large pot. Combine flour, water, eggs, salt, and parsley, mixing until ingredients are evenly distributed and flour is moist. Mixture need not be smooth. Drop from rounded tablespoon into the boiling water. Cook, uncovered, 15 minutes. Drain with slotted spoon and place in serving plate with stew.

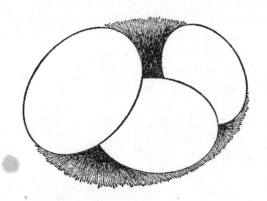

An unusual blend of fruits—yes, avocado is actually a fruit—with a creamy yoghurt topping.

CREAMY FRUIT SALAD

Yield: 4 servings
Preparation time: 5 to 10 minutes

1 small avocado, peeled and diced
1 large grapefruit, peeled and sectioned[3]
1 cup cantaloupe balls

Juice of ½ lemon
½ teaspoon salt
½ cup plain yoghurt
1 tablespoon honey

Combine fruit and sprinkle with lemon juice and salt. Chill until serving time. Beat yoghurt and honey together with a fork until smooth. At serving time top individual dishes of fruit salad with yoghurt dressing.

[3] Peel and section as you would an orange. See footnote 5, Fresh Fruit Cup for directions (see Index).

Menu #25

APRICOT NECTAR
STUFFED PEPPERS WITH ONIONS
CORN BREAD

Cooking Schedule: Apricot Nectar should be prepared at least 1 day before needed and can be refrigerated up to two weeks so you can always have some on hand.

Begin 1 hour before dinner and allow 40 minutes to prepare and bake Corn Bread and 20 minutes for the bread to cool before serving. Stuffed Peppers can be baked while the bread cools. Allow 10 minutes (while the bread is in the oven) to assemble peppers before baking. Tomato sauce is called for in the Stuffed Peppers so be sure you have some.

Bread can be baked early in the day if you wish and freezes well if you have leftovers for future meals.

Here is a beverage that will provide a nice change from the store-bought varieties. It stores well and can be kept in the refrigerator until needed. Use the apricots in cereals, puddings, muffins, or eat as they are for breakfast or dessert. Similar nectar can be made with dried prunes or peaches.

APRICOT NECTAR

Yield: 1½ cups per pound of fruit
Cooking time: 45 minutes

Cover dried apricots with water in saucepan allowing 2 pints water per pound of fruit. Cover and cook over low heat 45 minutes. Pour into large jar and refrigerate until desired. Then strain and serve in small glasses.

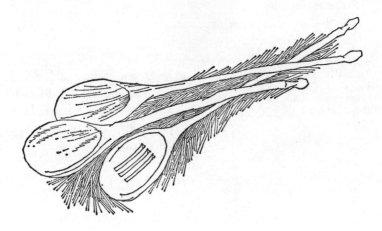

A quick corn bread with a surprisingly delicate crumb when made with fine corn meal; a coarser crumb with coarser meal. Ideal for sopping up sauces. Also good with butter and warm honey at breakfast or as a snack.

CORN BREAD

Utensils: 8-inch square baking pan
Preparation time: 5 minutes
Baking time: 35 minutes
Oven temperature: 400° F.

2 eggs, beaten
2 cups sour milk[1]
2 cups corn meal
2 teaspoons salt
1 tablespoon raw sugar or honey

3 teaspoons baking powder
¼ cup wheat germ
3 tablespoons oil or melted butter

[1] To make sour milk add 2 tablespoons lemon juice to 2 cups warm milk and let stand a minute.

Combine eggs and milk. Add dry ingredients, then liquid fat. Stir to blend. Pour into greased 8-inch square baking pan and bake in 400° F. oven 35 minutes. Cool before cutting.

This creamy blend of cheese and spinach in a green pepper shell makes a delicious main dish, easily prepared when you have some Basic Tomato Sauce on hand.

STUFFED PEPPERS WITH ONIONS

Yield: 2 servings
Preparation time: 10 minutes
Baking time: 20 minutes
Oven temperature: 350° F.

½ *pound raw spinach*
2 *green peppers*
8 *tiny white onions*
1 *cup (8 ounces) cottage cheese*
1 *egg*

½ *teaspoon salt*
Pepper
¼ *cup shredded Cheddar cheese*
2 *cups mild Mexican Tomato Sauce*[2]

Wash spinach and drain. Place in pot with only the water that clings to the leaves, cover and cook over low heat until wilted, about 3 minutes. Drain, if necessary, and chop. Slice top from pep-

[2] To make mild Mexican Tomato Sauce add ¼ teaspoon ground coriander and 1 tablespoon chili powder to Basic Tomato Sauce (see Index).

pers and remove seeds and white membrane. Place in saucepan with onions, pour boiling water over all, cover, and cook over low heat 5 minutes. Drain. While peppers boil, combine spinach, cottage cheese, egg, and salt. Stuff drained peppers with cheese mixture and place upright in a baking pan. Sprinkle liberally with pepper. Sprinkle 1 tablespoon Cheddar cheese on top of each pepper. Place onions around green peppers in the baking pan. Add remaining Cheddar cheese to sauce and pour over all. Bake in 350° F. oven 20 minutes.

Menu #26

HUMMUS AND PITA
BAKED STUFFED EGGPLANT
CRACKED WHEAT PILAF

Serving Suggestions: Many of the ingredients used in Mideastern cooking can be employed to turn out an assortment of vegetarian dishes. Common among these are chick peas, eggplant, cracked wheat, yoghurt, and sesame seeds. Cookbooks featuring this cuisine are a good source of ideas.

Cooking Schedule: Hummus can be prepared ahead of time and refrigerated; prepared while eggplant stuffing cooks; or made while eggplant is baking. It calls for cooked chick peas so be sure to have some on hand. The flavor becomes more pronounced as it stands.

Begin eggplant 1 hour before dinner, or prepare in advance and refrigerate filled shells until cooking time, 20 minutes before you want to eat.

Pilaf can cook while eggplant is in the oven.

Hummus is a dip or salad made from puréed cooked chick peas, flavored with garlic and tahini—a sesame seed paste. It is traditionally eaten with pieces of flat Mideastern pita bread which are used to scoop up the dip. It can be eaten on crackers or with a fork.

HUMMUS

Utensils: food mill
Yield: 3 cups; 4 servings
Preparation time: 5 to 10 minutes

2 cups cooked chick peas
¼ cup cooking liquid or water
¼ cup lemon juice
1½ to 2 teaspoons finely chopped garlic (2 to 3 cloves)

1¼ teaspoons salt
3 tablespoons tahini[1]
2 tablespoons chopped parsley
2 tablespoons olive oil, optional

[1] Tahini, a sesame seed paste, is available at Mideastern groceries, health food stores and gourmet shops. To make homemade Tahini, see Index.

[2] Mixture will thicken and the color will change as tahini is added.

Purée chick peas and liquid in food mill. Blend in lemon juice, garlic, and salt. Add tahini and mash mixture until smooth.[2] Place in flat soup plate or serving dish. Sprinkle parsley on top and pour the oil over the surface just before serving if desired.

A well-seasoned vegetable filling, including the pulp from the eggplant, is used to stuff the scooped-out shell of the vegetable. A melted cheese topping finishes off this filling main dish. Allow ½ eggplant per person.

STUFFED EGGPLANT

Utensils: large skillet; covered baking dish
Yield: 2 servings
Preparation time: 40 minutes
Baking time: 20 minutes
Oven temperature: 325° F.

1 eggplant	1 teaspoon dried basil
2 tablespoons oil	¾ teaspoon salt
1 onion, chopped	¼ teaspoon pepper
3 whole tomatoes, peeled[3]	½ cup grated Romano
1 cup diced celery	cheese
½ teaspoon oregano	

Wash eggplant, slice in half lengthwise, and scoop out pulp, leaving shell intact.[4] Dice pulp. Heat oil. Cook eggplant pulp,

[3] To peel tomatoes place in boiling water 1 minute or hold tomato over flame until it begins to blister on all

sides. Loosen peel with tip of knife and pull away from pulp.

[4] A curved grapefruit knife is a handy tool for removing vegetable pulp from shell.

onion, whole tomatoes, celery, and seasonings in hot oil 30 minutes, until mixture is thick and celery is tender. Stir occasionally. Stuff mixture into eggplant shells. Sprinkle ¼ cup grated cheese over each half. Place eggplant, filling side up, in shallow baking pan, and pour in ¼ to ½ inch boiling water—it should cover surface of pan entirely and bottom of eggplant. Cover and bake in 325° F. oven 10 minutes. Uncover and bake 10 minutes longer.

The grain for this dish is sold as cracked wheat, bulghur, or wheat pilaf. It can be served as a base for other foods or as a side dish. For a side dish allow about ½ cup cooked grain per person; as a base for a meal double the servings.

CRACKED WHEAT PILAF

Utensils: covered saucepan
Yield: 4 ½-cup servings
Preparation time: 5 minutes
Cooking time: 15 minutes

1 cup cracked wheat
1 small onion, chopped
1½ tablespoons oil

½ teaspoon salt
2 cups cooking liquid[5]

Sauté wheat and onion in oil until onion is transparent and wheat glazed. Add salt and liquid and bring to boil. Reduce heat, cover, and cook over lowest heat 15 minutes, until liquid is absorbed. Remove cover partially for steam to escape.[6]

[5] Use 2 cups water and 1 vegetable bouillon cube or 2 cups vegetable stock for richest flavor.

[6] To vary pilaf, add ¼ pound diced mushrooms when sautéing onion and wheat and increase oil to 2 tablespoons.

Menu #27

ILSA'S VEGETABLES IN CREAM SAUCE
BOILED POTATOES
LISA'S BREAD

Serving Suggestions: This meal is quickly put together, involves almost no cooking and is perfect for those days you're just not in the mood to do any work. Don't be misled though; it's good enough to serve to guests.

Cooking Schedule: If you don't have a loaf of bread in the freezer try this one. It's 3½ hours from start to finish, including rising and baking so begin early if you want it for dinner.

It takes 20 minutes to boil potatoes. The Vegetables in Cream Sauce can be prepared while they cook.

The addition of lots of dry milk to the recipe makes the protein content of this bread soar. This recipe produces a large loaf with a texture that's more tender than most. The baking of bread does not require much attention and is done in stages. Use the waiting periods to have breakfast, clean the house, read, or do whatever it is you do when you're home.

LISA'S BREAD

Utensils: 1 9×5×3-inch loaf pan
Yield: 1 loaf
Preparation time: 20 minutes
Rising time: 2½ hours
Baking time: 35 to 40 minutes
Oven temperature: 375° F.

1¼ cups warm water
1½ tablespoons (1½ packages) dry yeast
1 cup corn meal
1 teaspoon salt
2 tablespoons honey

1 egg or 2 egg yolks
1 cup dry milk powder
⅓ cup oil or melted butter
Approximately 4 cups whole wheat flour

Combine water, yeast, corn meal, salt, and honey in large bowl and let stand 10 minutes. Add egg, dry milk, oil, about 3½ cups flour, and mix well. Mixture will be dry. Cover with a cloth and let stand in a warm place 30 minutes. Turn dough on to a floured board or oilcloth and knead 10 minutes[1] adding remaining ½ cup flour as needed to prevent sticking. Grease large bowl and add dough, turning to coat all surfaces. Cover with cloth and let rise in warm place until doubled,

[1] For directions for kneading, and adding of flour see notes for Whole Wheat Rolls (see Index). While you're kneading 10 minutes seems like a long time—but this is one of the things that gives this bread its soft texture.

[2] See directions for shaping Oatmeal Bread (see Index).

[3] To test for doneness see directions for Oatmeal Bread (see Index).

[4] Brushing bread with water causes crust to steam and harden. If you prefer a soft crust wrap loaf in cloth until cool.

1 hour. Push dough down, shape,[2] and place seam side down in greased 9×5× 3-inch loaf pan. Cover and rise again until doubled, 45 minutes. Bake in 375° F. oven 35 to 40 minutes.[3] Remove from pan immediately and brush surface with water.[4]

BOILED POTATOES

Use two large potatoes for 4 servings. Scrub potatoes well, cut in half and divide each half into three pieces and place in pot with water to cover. Add a generous teaspoon salt and bring to boil. Cover, reduce heat, and cook about 20 minutes, until potatoes are tender but hold together. Drain completely. Peel can be removed easily with your fingers or the tip of a knife. To keep potatoes piping hot place in a bowl and cover with an inverted plate.

A tangy sour cream sauce provides the base for fresh vegetables. The sauce is cold and creamy and is served spooned over the hot potatoes.

ILSA'S VEGETABLES IN CREAM SAUCE

Yield: 4 servings
Preparation time: 10 minutes

1 onion, sliced
2 cups (1 pint) sour cream
½ cup wine vinegar[5]
6 tablespoons water
½ teaspoon salt
1 tomato, cut in bite-size pieces
6 radishes, sliced

1 small cucumber, quartered lengthwise, then cut into ¼-inch pieces[6]
½ sour pickle or half-sour pickle, quartered lengthwise, then cut into ¼-inch pieces

Place onion slices in small amount of water in saucepan, bring to boil and cook until wilted, about 2 minutes. Drain and run under cold water to cool. Combine sour cream, vinegar, water, and salt and stir until smooth. Mix in the vegetables. Serve immediately or refrigerate until serving time.

[5] The vinegar regulates the tanginess of the sauce. Less vinegar will produce a mild sauce. More vinegar will give the sauce more bite.

[6] If cucumber peel is waxed peel first.

Menu #28

CHEESE PUDDING
BROILED TOMATO
ZUCCHINI SALAD

Cooking Schedule: Prepare Zucchini Salad 1 to 3 days in advance. Preparation takes 10 minutes.

Begin Cheese Pudding just over 1 hour before dinner. Actual preparation time is about 15 minutes, but the pudding requires 40 minutes baking time and 10 minutes resting time before serving. It can be kept in the oven after heat is turned off if it is necessary to wait before dinner.

Prepare tomatoes 5 minutes before dinner, while Cheese Pudding cools.

Like many cold salads, the marination is the key to flavor. This one is worth planning a day or two ahead.

ZUCCHINI SALAD

Yield: 4 servings[1]
Preparation time: 10 to 15 minutes

4 medium zucchini	½ teaspoon salt
Oil	¼ teaspoon pepper
4 tablespoons vinegar	1 tablespoon dried basil
2 tablespoons oil	1 tablespoon chopped
1 clove garlic, chopped	parsley

Wash zucchini; do not peel. Trim ends. Cut zucchini into fingers 1½ inches long and ½ inch wide. Heat enough oil in large skillet to cover bottom. Add zucchini and fry until just tender on all sides. Drain on absorbent paper. Meanwhile, heat remaining ingredients in saucepan until mixture begins to boil. Remove from heat. Transfer zucchini to large jar, pour in heated dressing, cover, and chill overnight.[2] Keeps in refrigerator up to 4 days.[3]

[1] This salad can be prepared in any quantity desired. Use the proportion 2 parts vinegar to 1 part oil and vary amount of seasoning as necessary to give a pungent flavor.

[2] In a pinch, salad can be prepared 2 hours in advance of serving, but flavor will not be as well developed.

[3] Flavor becomes stronger as the salad stands.

BROILED TOMATO

Allow 1 small or ½ large tomato per person. Cut tomato in half crosswise, sprinkle cut surface with salt, pepper, and dried basil. Dot with butter and place under broiler heat 3 to 5 minutes, until butter melts and tomato is warmed through.

Similar in method to a soufflé, the result is heavier, not prone to collapse. The flavor is delicate, the texture moist and creamy.

CHEESE PUDDING

Utensils: Deep 2-quart casserole
Yield: 4 servings[4]
Preparation time: 10 minutes
Baking time: 40 minutes
Oven temperature: 350° F.

1 cup corn meal
1 cup cold milk
2 cups milk, heated to
   boiling
1 teaspoon salt

½ teaspoon dry mustard
1 cup (¼ pound) shredded
   Cheddar cheese
3 eggs, separated

[4] To serve 2: divide ingredients in half and use 2 eggs. Bake in 1-quart casserole. Baking time remains constant.

[5] Stir small amount of hot corn meal mixture into egg yolks initially and mix well to avoid coagulating the protein (cooking the yolks).

[6] To fold in egg whites see footnote 9, Cheese Soufflé (see Index).

Mix corn meal and cold milk in saucepan. Gradually add hot milk, stirring constantly. Cook over low heat, continuing to stir, 3 to 5 minutes, until thickened. Remove from heat. Add salt, mustard, and cheese. Stir until cheese is melted; if necessary return to low heat. Beat egg yolks. Gradually stir corn meal mixture into egg yolks.[5] Cool slightly. While cooling, beat egg whites until stiff peaks form. Do not overbeat. Fold into corn meal mixture gently, but thoroughly.[6] Pour into greased 2-quart casserole and bake in 350° F. oven 40 minutes, until puffed and delicately browned. Turn off heat and leave pudding in oven 10 minutes.

Menu #29

VEGETABLE PATTIES
GLAZED PARSNIPS
MUSHROOM BEAN SPROUT SALAD

Cooking Schedule: 35 to 40 minutes before dinner put parsnips on to cook. Then prepare the ingredients for the vegetable patties and mix them together; 20 minutes before dinner begin frying the patties and glaze the parsnips.

If you have time between the initial preparation and the cooking of the Vegetable Patties prepare the salad. You'll need about 5 minutes. Otherwise prepare the salad while the rest of the meal cooks.

These are thin vegetable pancakes well flavored with garlic and Tamari Soy Sauce. They can be made in any quantity.

VEGETABLE PATTIES

Utensils: large skillet
Yield: for every 2 servings
Preparation time: 10 minutes
Cooking time: 20 minutes

1 large carrot, grated
1 medium zucchini, grated
3 leaves spinach, chopped
2 scallions, chopped
6 tablespoons whole wheat
   flour
2 tablespoons wheat germ
1 egg, lightly beaten
1 clove garlic, crushed
1 tablespoon Tamari Soy
   Sauce
Oil for frying

Drain vegetables very well, then mix together. Stir in flour and wheat germ. Mix together egg, garlic, and soy sauce and add to vegetables. If mixture is watery add additional flour. Pour oil to cover surface of large skillet and heat. Spoon vegetable mixture into hot oil to make 4 pancakes. Cook over medium heat until brown and crisp, about 10 minutes. Turn and brown other side. Serve hot with additional Tamari soy sauce to taste.

GLAZED PARSNIPS

Utensils: covered saucepan
Yield: 4 servings
Preparation time: 5 minutes
Cooking time: 40 minutes, in two stages

6 parsnips
2 tablespoons butter
2 tablespoons honey

¼ cup apple juice or cider
1 teaspoon salt

Scrub parsnips and cook whole in covered saucepan in small amount of boiling water until almost tender, about 20 minutes. Drain and remove peel with tip of knife. Cut in half lengthwise, then crosswise into 2-inch pieces. Heat butter, honey, and cider in saucepan until butter melts and mixture is smooth. Add parsnips and salt and cook, basting occasionally over medium heat, until parsnips are glazed, about 20 minutes.

MUSHROOM BEAN SPROUT SALAD

Yield: 4 servings
Preparation time: 5 minutes

4 cups fresh bean sprouts
Boiling water
½ pound mushrooms, diced
  (1 cup)
1½ tablespoons Tamari Soy
  Sauce

4 teaspoons wine vinegar
4 teaspoons oil
¾ teaspoon salt
1 teaspoon raw sugar

Pour boiling water over bean sprouts, drain, and rinse with cold water. Drain again. Toss bean sprouts with mushrooms. Combine remaining ingredients and pour over vegetables. Let stand at room temperature until serving time.

Menu ✸30

Cooking Schedule: Cranberry Juice is another beverage you can prepare in advance and store in the refrigerator to use at will. It should be prepared at least 1 hour before serving and takes about 20 minutes to cook. It can be kept up to 2 weeks.

Prepare the Lentil-Barley Stew first, beginning 45 minutes before dinner. Additional preparation, about 5 to 10 minutes' worth, can take place after cooking begins. The stew can be prepared in advance and held at room temperature for a few hours or refrigerated up to 2 days. Reheat 5 to 10 minutes to serve.

The muffins can bake while the stew simmers. Allow 5 to 10 minutes to assemble them and 25 minutes for baking. They can be served warm or at room temperature, but should be allowed to cool slightly, about 10 minutes, before they are eaten.

You'll need 5 minutes to prepare the Vegetable Platter and Dressing and this can take place any time during the preparation of the rest of the meal.

CRANBERRY JUICE COCKTAIL

Yield: about 1 quart
Cooking time: 15 minutes

3 cups cranberries
4½ cups water

¾ cup honey
1½ tablespoons lemon juice

Wash cranberries, place in large saucepan with water, and cook over medium heat 15 minutes, until skins pop and cranberries are soft. Strain,[1] add honey to hot liquid, and stir until dissolved. Add lemon juice and chill at least 1 hour before serving. If not cold enough serve over ice.

[1] Use the cooked berries in breads, muffins, or fruit salads, or purée them, add honey to taste and serve in place of applesauce.

Lentils are an excellent source of protein. They are teamed here with barley and vegetables in a mild-flavored, filling stew. Leftovers can be reheated for lunch the next day.

LENTIL-BARLEY STEW

Utensils: large pot with cover
Yield: 6 servings
Preparation time: 5 to 10 minutes, simultaneous with cooking time
Cooking time: 45 minutes

1½ cups lentils	*4 stalks celery*
6 tablespoons whole barley	*2 small onions*
4½ cups water	*2½ teaspoons salt*
2 bay leaves	*6 whole cloves, optional*
3 carrots	

Wash lentils in cold water and drain. Place in pot with barley, water, and bay leaves and bring to boil. Reduce heat, cover, and cook over low heat 45 minutes. Meanwhile peel carrots if necessary and cut into 1-inch pieces; cut celery into 1½-inch pieces (including tops); cut onions in quarters. After lentils and barley have been cooking 20 minutes add the vegetables, the salt, and the cloves, cover, and continue to cook until the 45 minutes are up. Vegetables should be tender but not mushy.

These muffins are ideal with stews or with butter or cream cheese for breakfast. They are coarse-grained and just sweet enough . . . one of the best.

RYE MUFFINS

Utensils: muffin (or cupcake) pan
Yield: 9 muffins
Preparation time: 5 minutes
Baking time: 25 minutes
Oven temperature: 375° F.

1½ cups rye flour	¼ cup molasses
½ teaspoon baking soda	1 egg
½ teaspoon salt	2 tablespoons water
¼ cup oil	¼ cup chopped raisins

Combine flour, baking soda and salt and stir well. Beat together oil, molasses, egg and water and add with raisins to the flour. Stir only enough to moisten all ingredients. Spoon batter into 9 oiled muffin cups, handling as little as possible. Bake in a 375° F. oven 25 minutes. Cool slightly in pan before serving.

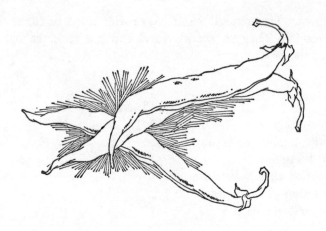

RAW VEGETABLE PLATTER WITH
CREAMY TOMATO DRESSING

[2] To trim green beans wash thoroughly, then snap ends with fingers as close to the tip as they will break easily. Do not use a knife.

Prepare a platter of raw carrot sticks, celery stalks, cauliflowerets, and trimmed green beans.[2] Place in center of table for everyone to help themselves. Pass a Creamy Tomato Dressing made by combining, for every two servings, ¼ cup tomato juice, 2 tablespoons cottage cheese, ½ tablespoon lemon juice, and ¼ teaspoon curry powder in blender container and puréeing on low speed until smooth.

DESSERTS

Most of the doubts we have about the foods we do eat have been centered on those foods we consider desserts. Dessert is regarded as the "Forbidden Sweet"—an indulgence rather than an integral part of the meal.

Feel guilty no longer! There is an enormous variety of desserts that are both a nice way to end a meal and wholesome, ranging from the simple to the elaborate.

Among the easiest and best for you are fresh fruits in season, dried fruits, and nuts. These require no preparation and can be kept on hand at all times. In the European style, crackers and cheese are always welcome after dinner or for evening snacking. To satisfy a sweet tooth with very little effort fresh bread spread with honey and warmed in the oven or under the broiler is ideal. In addition to these easy-to-prepare desserts, most health food stores offer a wide range of cookies made with whole grains and natural sweeteners that look and taste like the real old-fashioned kind.

When preparing more elaborate desserts at home just remember to incorporate fresh fruits (and also vegetables), nuts and dried fruits for flavor and sweetening; try homemade puddings and custards thickened with eggs or potato starch flour; raw, unrefined sugar can always replace white sugar in a recipe and honey, molasses, and pure maple syrup should be substituted whenever possible. Whole grain flours should always be used for baking and can be used in various combinations—soy flour and potato starch flour can be combined with whole wheat flour for a more tender product, rolled oats add interest to the flavor and texture of many baked goods, and dry milk powder can be added to the flour to increase the protein content of many cakes and cookies.

Here are some recipes from my kitchen to get you started, a

smattering in the many areas of fruit, puddings, cookies and cakes, and nonsweet dessert choices. You can add to this list by varying conventional fruit and pudding recipes found in all general cookbooks with the more nutritious ingredients you are now buying. Experiment with cookies, cakes, and pies. Many cuisines outside our own feature sweet vegetable puddings and grain desserts, so you might consult foreign cookbooks for more exotic fare. Don't be afraid to explore and experiment, and you'll find a vast collection of recipes there for you to enjoy.

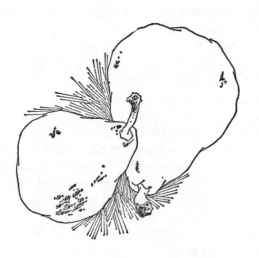

MAPLE ALMOND MERINGUES

Utensils: baking sheet
Yield: 10 large cookies
Baking time: 55 minutes
Oven temperature: 275° F.

2 egg whites
⅓ cup maple syrup
½ teaspoon vanilla

¼ cup finely chopped
almonds

Beat egg whites until soft peaks form. Gradually add maple syrup and continue to beat until stiff peaks form. Fold in vanilla and chopped almonds. Cover a baking sheet with foil or unglazed brown paper. Drop meringue by soupspoonfuls onto the lined baking sheet. Depress the center of each with the back of the spoon. Place in 275° F. oven for 45 minutes, reduce heat to 250°, and bake 10 minutes longer. Allow meringues to cool on the paper, then remove gently, or, if foil is used, peel off. Store in a covered tin. These cookies can be kept, properly stored, at least 1 week.

MOLASSES BARS

Utensils: greased 11×7-inch or 9-inch square baking pan
Yield: about 35 cookies
Baking time: 25 to 30 minutes
Oven temperature: 350° F.

2 eggs
¼ cup raw (unrefined) sugar
½ cup molasses
1 teaspoon vanilla
1 cup whole wheat graham
  cracker crumbs

1 cup coarsely chopped
  pecans
½ cup raisins

Combine all ingredients and stir well to blend. Spread into a greased 11×7-inch or 9-inch square baking pan and bake in 350° F. oven 25 to 30 minutes. Cut into bars 1×2 inches and cool in pan.

DATE SQUARES

Utensils: greased 9-inch square baking pan
Yield: 25 to 30 squares
Baking time: 20 to 25 minutes
Oven temperature: 350° F.

1 cup whole wheat flour	¼ teaspoon salt
1 cup rolled oats	⅓ cup oil
1 teaspoon baking soda	¼ cup honey
½ teaspoon cinnamon	Date Filling (recipe follows)
¼ teaspoon cloves	

Mix dry ingredients together. Stir in oil with a fork, then honey. Press ½ of the dough flat with the palm of the hand and use it to line the bottom of a greased 9-inch square baking pan. Spread Date Filling over dough. Pat remaining dough into a thin layer and press onto filling to cover. Bake at 350° F. until browned, 20 to 25 minutes. Cool slightly, cut into small squares, and finish cooling in pan. These cookies are very rich, so the squares can be cut small. The cookies will store well in a covered tin.

DATE FILLING: To make the filling for these cookies combine 1 cup chopped dates and ¼ cup water in a small saucepan. Cook over very low heat until thick, about 5 minutes. Remove from heat and stir in 2 tablespoons honey.

WALNUT COOKIES

Utensils: ungreased baking sheet
Yield: about 40 cookies
Baking time: 10 minutes
Oven temperature: 375° F.

1 cup whole wheat flour	½ cup honey
½ teaspoon baking soda	½ teaspoon vanilla
½ teaspoon salt	1 egg
⅓ cup oil	1 cup chopped walnuts

Combine dry ingredients. Combine oil, honey, vanilla, and egg and add to dry ingredients, mixing until smooth. Fold in nuts. Drop cookies by teaspoonfuls onto an ungreased baking sheet about 1 inch apart. Bake at 375° F. until lightly browned, about 10 minutes. Remove immediately from baking sheet and cool on wire rack. For variety substitute ½ cup chopped raisins for half of the nuts.

FRUIT TURNOVERS

Utensils: ungreased baking sheet
Yield: 9 small turnovers
Baking time: 10 minutes
Oven temperature: 400° F.

1 cup whole wheat flour	1½ tablespoons honey
¼ teaspoon salt	Fruit Fillings (recipes
¼ cup oil	follow)
½ cup cottage cheese	¼ teaspoon cinnamon

Combine flour and salt in bowl and stir in oil with a fork till tiny pea-like balls are formed. Combine cottage cheese and honey and mix into dough until evenly blended. Place ¼ of the dough on a lightly floured board, cover with waxed paper, and roll thin. Lift paper and cut into 4-inch squares. Slip thin blade of knife under each square to lift from board. Continue, using all dough. Place a small amount of filling on half of each square and fold remaining half of dough over the filling to form a triangle. Press edges together with tines of fork to seal. Sprinkle with cinnamon. Place on ungreased baking sheet. For apple turnovers, make a small slit in top of dough to allow steam to escape during baking. Bake in 400° F. oven 10 minutes. Cool slightly and serve warm, or allow to cool and then reheat turnover in a 300° F. oven 5 minutes before serving if you wish.

FRUIT FILLINGS: *Banana*—For every 6 turnovers slice 1 banana thinly and place slices on dough. Top with 3 raisins each. *Apple*—Combine 1 medium apple, peeled and thinly sliced, ½ teaspoon cinnamon, ¼ teaspoon nutmeg, and 2 tablespoons honey. Use to fill 6 turnovers.

NO-BAKE FRUIT BARS

Yield: 32 bars

1 cup raisins
1 cup assorted dried fruit
½ cup almonds
¼ cup dry milk powder

¼ cup whole wheat graham
 cracker crumbs
¼ cup molasses

Chop fruit and nuts. Combine with milk powder, graham cracker crumbs, then add molasses and mix well. Pinch off a heaping teaspoon and roll into 1-inch bars. These cookies can be stored indefinitely in a plastic bag or wrapped in foil in the refrigerator.

DROP DOUGHNUTS

Utensils: frying thermometer; deep pot
Yield: about 20 doughnuts
Frying time: 1 to 2 minutes
Frying temperature: 350° F.

1 tablespoon (1 package)
   dry yeast
¼ cup warm water
¼ cup milk, scalded
2 tablespoons honey or raw
   sugar
½ teaspoon salt
¼ teaspoon nutmeg

½ teaspoon cinnamon
2 tablespoons butter or oil
1½ cups whole wheat flour
1 egg
Oil for deep-fat frying
Additional raw sugar and
   cinnamon

Add yeast to water and let stand about 5 minutes until dissolved. Pour milk into a bowl and add honey, nutmeg, cinnamon, and butter or oil. Add ¾ cup flour and beat until smooth. Beat in egg and yeast. Add remaining flour and beat until smooth. Cover with a clean cloth and let rise in a warm place until doubled, 2 to 3 hours. Stir down, cover, and let rest 45 minutes (or longer if need be according to your time schedule). Pour oil into a deep pot to reach ⅓ the depth and heat to 350° F. Drop dough by the soupspoonful, a few spoonfuls at a time, into the hot fat. Doughnuts will sink initially, then rise. Cook until doughnuts are golden, about 1 minute, then drain on absorbent paper. Combine sugar and cinnamon in a paper bag, add doughnuts, a few at a time, and shake to coat. Serve doughnuts immediately or within the next few hours; they do not keep more than a day.

WHOLE WHEAT GINGERBREAD

Utensils: greased 8-inch square baking pan
Yield: 16 gingerbread squares
Baking time: 40 minutes
Oven temperature: 350° F.

1 cup molasses	*1 teaspoon ginger*
½ cup oil or butter	*½ teaspoon cinnamon*
½ cup boiling water	*¼ teaspoon nutmeg*
1¼ cups whole wheat flour	*1 egg*
2 teaspoons baking powder	*¼ cup raisins coated with*
¼ teaspoon baking soda	*whole wheat flour*

Beat together molasses and oil. Add boiling water, and, if using butter instead of oil, stir until melted. Mix together dry ingredients and add to molasses mixture. Beat egg, then beat into batter. Stir in raisins. Pour batter (it will be quite thin) into a greased 8-inch square baking pan and bake in 350° F. oven 40 minutes. Cool in pan and cut into 2-inch squares before transferring gingerbread to a plate. Serve if desired with whipped cream or Whipped Topping.

WHIPPED TOPPING: Combine ½ cup dry milk powder and ½ cup ice water in a chilled bowl. Beat with an electric or rotary beater until soft peaks form, 5 minutes. Add 2 tablespoons orange juice, 2 tablespoons honey or raw sugar if desired, and continue beating another 5 minutes until fluffy. Keep in refrigerator until serving time, and use within 2 hours. If held longer topping will begin to soften and separate.

FRUITCAKE

Utensils: well greased 6-cup ring mold or tube pan
Yield: 1 cake
Baking time: 1 hour
Oven temperature: 300° F.

½ *pound pitted dates*	½ *teaspoon baking powder*
½ *pound dried apples*	¼ *teaspoon salt*
1 *cup dried apricots*	3 *eggs*
1 *cup walnut halves*	½ *cup molasses*
¾ *cup whole wheat flour*	1 *teaspoon vanilla*
¼ *cup raw sugar*	

Mix together dates, apples, apricots, and nuts. Combine flour, sugar, baking powder, and salt and add to fruit mixture. Stir well. Beat eggs, then beat in molasses and vanilla. Add to fruit mixture and stir until all ingredients are moistened. Spoon into a well-greased 6-cup ring mold or tube pan and bake in a 300° F. oven 1 hour. Cool in pan 5 to 10 minutes, then turn out onto a wire rack and cool completely. This cake stores very well and wrapped in foil will retain its moistness and delicate flavor, making it ideal for gift-giving or mailing at holiday time.

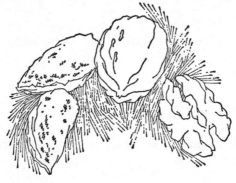

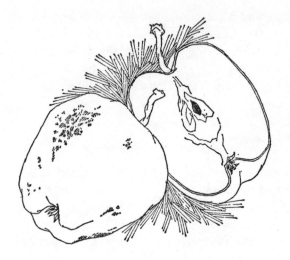

MACAROON TOP APPLE CAKE

Utensils: greased 9-inch baking dish or glass pie plate
Yield: 6 servings
Baking time: 50 minutes
Oven temperature: 375° F.

  4 cups peeled sliced apples
  ¼ cup honey
  ¼ teaspoon cinnamon

Place sliced apples in a greased 9-inch baking dish or glass pie plate. Add honey and cinnamon and stir to coat slices. Bake for 20 minutes in 375° F. oven; meanwhile prepare the topping.

  ½ cup raw sugar or ¼ cup   *½ teaspoon baking powder*
    honey and ¼ cup raw   *¼ teaspoon salt*
    sugar   *½ cup whole wheat flour*
  2 tablespoons butter   *½ teaspoon vanilla*
  1 egg, lightly beaten

Cream sugar and butter until smooth. Add beaten egg, dry ingredients and vanilla, stir until smooth and spread over the surface of the hot apples. Return to 375° F. oven for about 30 minutes, until the crust is golden brown. Cut into squares or wedges and serve warm or cold.

PUMPKIN PIE

Utensils: 9-inch pie plate
Yield: 1 9-inch pie
Baking time: 55 minutes
Oven temperatures: 450° F.; 350° F.

1½ cups mashed cooked
   pumpkin
½ teaspoon salt
1 cup milk
2 eggs, beaten
½ cup molasses
2 tablespoons raw sugar

1 teaspoon cinnamon
½ teaspoon nutmeg
¼ teaspoon ginger
½ teaspoon vanilla
Walnut Pie Crust (recipe
   follows)

Combine ingredients in the order given and pour into unbaked pie crust. Bake in 450° F. oven 15 minutes, reduce temperature to 350° F., and bake an additional 40 minutes, until almost set. Remove from oven and cool. Delicious with ice cream, whipped cream, or whipped topping as well as plain.

WALNUT PIE CRUST: Combine ¾ cup ground walnuts, ½ cup whole wheat flour, 2 tablespoons oil, and 2 tablespoons raw sugar and press into a 9-inch pie plate.

PECAN PIE

Utensils: 9-inch pie plate
Yield: 1 9-inch pie
Baking time: 35 minutes
Oven temperatures: 400° F.; 350° F.

½ cup honey	1 cup broken pecans
½ cup raw sugar	Whole Wheat Pie Crust
¼ cup butter	(recipe follows)
3 eggs, beaten	

Mix honey and sugar in small saucepan and cook over low heat until smooth. Add butter and stir until melted. Cool slightly, then add beaten eggs and nuts. Pour into unbaked pie crust. Bake at 400° F. 10 minutes, reduce heat to 350° F. and continue baking 25 minutes, until set. Cool before serving.

Whole Wheat Pie Crust: With a fork stir ¼ cup oil and 2 tablespoons cold water into 1⅓ cups whole wheat flour until flour is just moistened and holds together when pressed into a ball. Dough will be crumbly. Turn out onto a floured board or oilcloth and roll thin to fit a 9-inch pie plate. Fit dough to pan and flute edges.

BANANES AUX PECANS

Utensils: greased 1-quart baking dish
Yield: 6 servings
Cooking time: 10 minutes

4 bananas	*6 tablespoons molasses*
1 cup chopped pecans	*1 tablespoon butter*

Slice bananas in half crosswise; slice each half lengthwise to make 4 slices, or 32 slices in all. Layer half of the bananas in a greased 1-quart baking dish, spread pecans over, and top with remaining banana slices. Pour molasses over all, cut butter into tiny cubes, and place over the top. Broil for 10 minutes, 6 inches from the heat, until bananas begin to brown. Serve warm.

MANGO JAM

Yield: 2½ to 3 cups; 6 servings

4 small mangoes	*Rind and juice of 1 medium*
½ cup honey	*lemon*
1 cup water	

Peel mangoes and slice meat from pit. Combine honey, water, lemon rind and juice in saucepan and bring to boil. Add fruit and cook over low heat until thickened, about 20 minutes. Pour into a jar and chill. Serve jam very cold with crackers and slices of mild white cheese, such as mozzarella. Jam can be stored in the refrigerator several weeks.

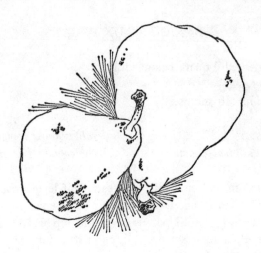

GINGER PEARS

Utensils: covered baking dish
Yield: 2 servings
Baking time: 1½ to 2 hours
Oven temperature: 300° F.

1 *large Anjou pear*	½ *stick cinnamon*
1½ *tablespoons honey*	2 *tablespoons water*
¼ *teaspoon ginger*	

Slice pear in half lengthwise and remove core. Place in a baking dish cut side up. Spread honey over cut surface and sprinkle with ginger. Place a piece of cinnamon on each half; put water in bottom of baking dish. Cover tightly and bake in 300° F. oven 1 hour. Turn pear over so skin side is up, baste lightly with syrup, cover and bake an additional 30 minutes to 1 hour, until fork-tender. Serve warm or cold with light cream or warm honey flavored with ginger if desired.

UKRAINIAN CHEESE PANCAKES

Utensils: food mill or sieve
Yield: 16 to 20 small cakes; 4 servings

2 cups cottage cheese,
well drained
2 eggs
¼ teaspoon salt
2 tablespoons honey

½ cup whole wheat flour
1 to 2 tablespoons butter
4 tablespoons pure fruit
preserves or jam

Purée cheese in food mill or force through sieve with a wooden spoon. Beat in eggs, salt, honey, and flour. Melt 1 tablespoon of the butter in a large skillet. Drop the batter by rounded tablespoons into the hot butter and fry, 4 at a time, until browned, about 5 minutes. Turn and brown the other side, about 3 minutes over a fairly low heat. Add additional butter to the pan as needed. Serve the cheese cakes hot topped with preserves.

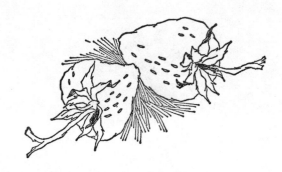

FRUIT CREAM

Utensils: food mill or sieve
Yield: 4 servings

1 *small apple*
1 *pear*
1 *small orange, peeled*
6 *cherries, sliced in half with pits removed*
2 *to 3 teaspoons lemon juice*

½ *cup cottage cheese*
2 *tablespoons milk*
2 *tablespoons honey*
2 *tablespoons grated nuts*

Dice apple, pear, and orange, add cherries and sprinkle lemon juice over all. Purée cheese in food mill or press through sieve with wooden spoon. Beat in milk and honey with a fork until smooth. Divide fruit into 4 dishes, top with "cream" and grated nuts.

INDIAN PUDDING

Utensils: greased 1-quart baking dish
Yield: 4 servings
Baking time: 1 to 1½ hours
Oven temperature: 350° F.

⅓ cup yellow corn meal
2 cups (1 pint) milk
1 tablespoon butter
¼ cup molasses
⅓ cup raw sugar
¼ teaspoon ginger

½ teaspoon salt
½ teaspoon cinnamon
1 egg, beaten
¼ cup raisins, optional
½ cup cold milk

Combine corn meal and 1 cup milk in saucepan and mix until smooth. Add the other cup of milk and cook over medium heat until mixture has been thickened for 2 minutes. Add butter. Mix molasses, sugar, spices, and egg and add to hot mixture, stirring well to prevent egg from cooking. Stir in raisins, which are optional but recommended. Pour mixture into a greased 1-quart baking dish, pour the cold milk over the top, and bake in a 350° F. oven until just set and browned on top, 1 to 1½ hours. Serve warm or at room temperature. Especially delicious topped with pure vanilla ice cream (homemade or available at health food stores).

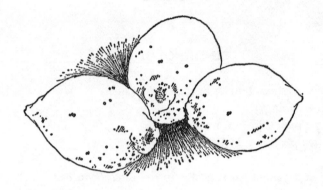

SWEET POTATO PUDDING WITH LEMON SAUCE

Utensils: greased 2-quart casserole
Yield: 6 to 8 servings
Baking time: 1½ to 2 hours
Oven temperature: 350° F.

> 4 large sweet potatoes (7 or
>   8 cups grated)
> 2 eggs
> 1 cup molasses
>
> ½ cup milk
> 1 cup butter, melted
> ½ teaspoon salt

Peel and grate potatoes and drain well. Beat eggs; add molasses, milk, melted butter, and salt. Stir in grated potato. Turn into a greased 2-quart casserole and bake in a 350° F. oven 1½ to 2 hours, until pudding is very dark. Serve warm with Lemon Sauce.

LEMON SAUCE:

> 1 cup water
> 1 tablespoon potato starch
>   flour
>
> ½ cup honey
> Rind and juice of 1 lemon

Combine 1 tablespoon of the water with the potato starch to make a smooth paste. Combine remaining water and honey in saucepan and heat until smooth. Add flour paste and cook over low heat, stirring constantly until mixture is thickened and comes to a boil. Remove from heat immediately and stir in lemon juice and rind. Serve warm or chilled.

BROWN RICE PUDDING

Utensils: greased 1½-quart baking dish
Yield: 6 to 8 servings
Baking time: 45 minutes
Oven temperature: 325° F.

1½ cups soft cooked brown rice[1]
2 eggs
1 cup milk
Juice and rind of 1 orange
¼ teaspoon salt

5 tablespoons honey
1 tablespoon butter
½ teaspoon vanilla
½ cup chopped dried apricots

Beat eggs and combine with milk, orange juice and rind, salt, honey, butter, and vanilla. Fold in rice and apricots gently, but well. Pour into a greased 1½-quart baking dish and bake in a 325° F. oven until set, about 45 minutes. Serve warm or cold.

[1] FOR SOFT COOKED RICE wash ½ cup raw brown rice in cold water and drain well. Place in saucepan, add 1½ cups water and bring to boil, cover, reduce heat to lowest point and cook 45 minutes, until all water is absorbed.

ROASTED CHICK PEA NUTS

Utensils: shallow baking pan
Yield: 2 cups
Baking time: 1 hour
Oven temperature: 350° F.

1 cup dried chick peas	*2 tablespoons oil*
3 cups water	*1 teaspoon salt*

Place chick peas in pot with water, bring to boil for 2 minutes, remove from heat and let stand 1 hour. Drain peas and spread on absorbent paper to dry. Spread chick peas out in shallow baking pan, sprinkle with oil, and shake to coat. Bake peas at 350° F. 1 hour, until lightly browned, shaking the pan occasionally. Drain on absorbent paper and shake with the salt in a paper bag. Serve in a bowl so people can help themselves. Keeps for weeks.

"SNACKS"

For dessert and snacking make up a batch of "Snacks" and store them in an airtight container, to be used as desired. The proportions are to taste but this is the idea: Combine a couple of cups of sunflower seeds with a quarter as much sesame seeds. Add about a cup of raw cashews and raw almonds, a cup of raisins, and about the same amount of chopped dates. You can add some wheat germ, roasted soy beans, carob bits, or additional nuts or dried fruit as you see fit. Place in bowls around the room for everyone to enjoy.

CREATING A MENU OF YOUR OWN

Now that you are well into the natural foods way of life, you will undoubtedly have no trouble adding some menus of your own. You can repeat the menus here if you like, rearranging similar items for variety to create a new pattern.

When designing menus of your own remember to include at least one protein rich food on the menu: Cheese, milk, eggs, nuts, dried beans, or whole grain products.

Choose a wide assortment of fruits and vegetables to obtain all important vitamins and minerals.

Winter menus can be built around hearty soups with rice, barley, beans, or potatoes added for extra nourishment. These make satisfying meals served with chunks of whole grain bread and cheese.

Cold soups, crackers, and vegetable salads are ideal choices on warm summer days.

Mixed vegetable plates, baked potatoes with cottage cheese, vegetable-cheese casseroles, hearty salads with cheese or eggs, macaroni or noodles and cheese, pasta and vegetable sauces, the many varieties of eggs, grains, stuffed vegetables, bean casseroles, and sandwiches are all good focal points for your own menus.

III

Natural Food Expertise

COOKING HINTS

Read the recipe through once before you begin.

Organizing your kitchen makes cooking simpler, faster, and helps eliminate mistakes. Assemble all ingredients before you begin to cook. This will cut preparation time down appreciably.

When ingredients list calls for food to be chopped, beaten, etc., do this first. "Preparation time" includes these operations. A recipe may take a bit longer the first time, but as you become familiar with it you can proceed at a faster pace, developing short cuts of your own.

When oil is called for in cooking, the variety used is up to you. For information about oil consult "Salad Dressings" in the section SHOPPING FOR FOOD.

When using the oven preheat it about 10 minutes before you begin baking to bring it to the desired temperature.

When cooking on the range be sure to follow recipe directions for heat intensity.

SELECTION AND CARE OF VEGETABLES

Vegetable	Season	Selection	Storage	Preparation
Artichoke	Year round Peak: Mar.-May Low: July-Aug.	Compact, tightly closed heads, heavy in relation to size. Large clinging leaves. Freshness indicated by green color. Size unrelated to quality or flavor.	Store in refrigerator covered up to 4 days. Use as soon as possible.	Trim stem leaving about ¼" stub. Trim tough tips of leaves with scissors and remove tough leaves at base. Wash in cold water to prevent darkening. Prepare just before cooking and add lemon juice to water. Darkens rapidly.
Asparagus	Mar.-June	2 lbs. for 4 servings. Firm, well-rounded stalks with compact tips. Flat stalks are tough and stringy.	Store in vegetable crisper or plastic bag in refrigerator 2-4 days. Use as soon as possible.	Break stalk as far down as it snaps easily. Discard ends. Remove scales with knife, if desired. Wash thoroughly.
Avocado	Year round Peak: Dec.-Apr.	Ready to eat when it "gives" slightly when squeezed; heavy, uniform color, no cracks.	Store at room temperature until soft enough to eat. Once ripe can store in refrigerator 2-4 weeks whole, 1-2 days cut.	Peel, cut in half, and twist halves slightly to get them apart. Remove pit. Sprinkle with lemon juice to prevent darkening.
Beets	Year round Peak: June-Aug.	2 bunches serve 4. Medium size beets, smooth and firm. Avoid any with soft wet areas (decay) or shriveled rough texture (tough). Fresh tops.	Store in vegetable crisper or plastic bag up to 2 weeks in refrigerator. Remove tops (not tips), leaving 2".	Wash thoroughly and trim stem, leaving 1-2 inches before cooking. Peel and remove tops after cooking (slip off with tip of knife). Otherwise red color will run out.
Broccoli	Year round Peak: Oct.-Dec. Low: July-Aug.	Firm tender stalks with dark green or purplish green compact clusters of buds. Touches of yellow indicate buds are beginning to blossom and stalks will be tough and stringy.	Store in vegetable crisper or plastic bag in refrigerator up to 1 week.	Trim leaves and tough bottom of stem. Soak in cold salted water. If stalks are thick slit lengthwise almost to flower to speed cooking.

Brussels Sprouts	Sept.-Feb.	Green, compact, bright, with no yellow spots or worm holes. Firm. Small to medium are best.	Store in vegetable crisper or plastic bag in refrigerator 4 days.	Remove loose or discolored leaves; cut off tip of stem. Wash.
Cabbage	Year round	1 head, 1½ lbs. for 4. Heads firm and hard, heavy in relation to size with good color and no outer blemishes.	Remove any discolored leaves. Store in plastic bag in refrigerator 1-2 weeks.	Do not cut until just before using. Wash, discard wilted leaves only, and remove core, leaving only enough to hold leaves intact. If shredding, use knife, not chopper, to retain more vitamin C.
Carrots	Year round	Firm, smooth, well shaped, and colored with fresh, green tops.	Remove tops, they only drain moisture from root. Store in plastic bag or vegetable crisper in refrigerator 1-2 weeks.	Trim ends and scrub. Peel only if old and skins are tough.
Cauliflower	Year round Peak: Sept.-Nov. Low: May-Aug.	Compact solid head with close creamy white clusters and fresh green outer leaves.	Store in plastic bag in refrigerator 3-5 days.	Remove outer leaves and soak in cold salted water to remove any lurking bugs.
Celery	Year round	Crisp thick stalks that snap easily, topped with fresh leaves.	Store in crisper or plastic bag in refrigerator 3-5 days. Stand in ice cold water to crisp if necessary.	Trim leaves and root end. Scrub well. Use leaves in salad.
Corn	Peak: May-Sept.	Choose well-filled ears with plump milky kernels, covered with husks of good green color. Just picked if possible.	Store uncovered, in husks, in refrigerator 1-2 days. Use as soon as possible.	Remove husks and silk just before cooking.
Cucumber	Year round	Firm, bright, well shaped. Medium or dark green in color, unwaxed.	Keeps in vegetable crisper in refrigerator about 1 week.	Trim ends. Wash. Do not peel unless skin is extraordinarily tough or waxed.

Vegetable	Season	Selection	Storage	Preparation
Eggplant	Year round	Firm, heavy for size, free from scars, with uniform rich purple color. Dark brown spots indicate decay.	Store at cool room temperature in plastic bag to prevent drying out 1-2 days, or in refrigerator.	Trim ends, wash. Do not peel unless skin is tough. Do not soak or sprinkle with salt and let stand to drain as is often suggested, as this removes valuable minerals.
Garlic	Year round	Firm roots with unbroken sheath.	Store in cool dry place in small wire or plastic open basket. Do not refrigerate.	Remove individual clove. Remove protective coating, then mince or crush.
Green Beans	May-Oct. Peak: June	1½ lbs. for 4 servings. Young, crisp pods without bumps. Snap easily, no rust.	Keep in plastic bag in refrigerator 3-5 days. Use as soon as possible.	Rinse, trim ends. Break in 1″ lengths, lengthwise, or leave whole. Snap by hand rather than cutting with knife whenever possible.
Leeks	Year round Peak: Sept., Nov., and spring	Crisp with green fresh tops and medium-sized necks.	Store in refrigerator up to 1 week.	Wash thoroughly to remove sand, trim root end and tops to leave 1″ of green. If unavailable substitute green onions or scallions.
Lettuce	Year round	*Crisphead* (Western Iceberg or Iceberg) Firm, heavy with crisp leaves. *Butterhead* (Boston) Soft head with oily feeling inner leaves. *Bibb* (Small, cup shape) Deep green outer leaves. *Cos or Romaine* Elongated head, stiff upright leaves.	Rinse well, don't soak, and drain. Remove damaged leaves only. Store in crisper or plastic bag in refrigerator for up to 3-5 days.	Tear with hands, rather than knife to prevent darkening at cut edges.
Mushrooms	Year round Peak: Nov.–Dec. Low: Aug.	Firm and white. Darkening does not necessarily mean decay, but may indicate bruising. Best when no gills visible between stem and cap.	Refrigerate in plastic bag 1-2 days. *or* Lay on shallow tray or rack and cover with damp paper towel. Refrigerate this way 1 week.	Wash but do not soak and trim stem end. Cut just before using to prevent darkening.

Onions	Year round	Hard, well-shaped with dry skins.	Store at cool room temperature in open mesh bag. Keep several months in dry place. Keep a few for immediate use in refrigerator to reduce tears when peeling and cutting.	Trim ends. Remove outer layer. To reduce weeping you can do this under cold running water. To chop cut into halves crosswise, with sharp knife, cube cut surface by cutting horizontally and vertically almost to intact end. Then cut crosswise to release cubes.
Parsley	Year round	Bright green, free from wilting and yellowing.	Wash. Store in refrigerator with stems in cold water or in closed container 3-5 days. Can be chopped and frozen in plastic bag for future cooking.	Wash, trim tough stems. Use scissors to chop.
Parsnips	Year round	1½ lbs. for 4 servings. Smooth, firm, well shaped, of small to medium size.	Store in refrigerator 1-2 weeks.	To retain sweet nutty flavor steam, do not boil, in peel. After cooking remove peel with point of knife.
Peas	May-Aug.	2 lbs. for 4 servings. Young, freshly picked. Pod should be bright green, velvety to touch, and well filled. Underdeveloped peas have flat dark pods with wilted look. Overdeveloped pods are swollen with flecked, yellowish-green color. Old peas have yellowish color and are tough with poor flavor.	Store uncovered in pods in refrigerator 1-2 days in coldest section.	Leave in shell until ready to serve. If eating raw, serve in pod and let everyone shell his own.
Scallion	Year round	Crisp green tops with well-formed necks.	Store in plastic bag in refrigerator up to 1 week.	Remove outer skin. Trim root end and top to leave 1" of green.

Vegetable	Season	Selection	Storage	Preparation
Spinach	Year round	Good color with large tender leaves, not wilted or bruised.	Rinse well, several times, drain and remove blemished leaves. Store in crisper or plastic bag 3-5 days.	Remove root and tough stems.
Squash, Summer and Zucchini	Year round Peak: May-July	Good color, heavy for size with soft rind you can puncture with fingernail.	Store in crisper in refrigerator 3-8 days.	Wash. Trim ends, do not peel.
Winter	Acorn and Butternut year round Others: Aug.-July	Hard intact shell, no soft spots. Thick rind, bright color. 3 lbs. for 4 servings.	Cool dry place, several months.	Cut in half. Scoop out seeds. Bake in rind, but do not eat rind.
Sweet Pepper	Year round Slight peak: May-Aug.	Firm, bright, shiny with thick flesh and strong color (red or green). Crooked shape is fine but may have more waste.	Store in vegetable crisper in refrigerator 3-5 days.	Wash. Remove seeds and inner membrane.
Potatoes	Year round	Firm, smooth, shallow eyed, free from growth cracks and soft spots and eyes. Regular shape.	Store in dark, dry place at room temperature in small quantities. Larger amounts in cool moist place like cellar, several months. "New" potatoes spoil quicker. Cooked in refrigerator 4-5 days.	Scrub well. Cook in skins and remove skin, if desired, after cooking, with point of knife. If peeled before cooking keep in cool water to prevent darkening.

Pumpkin	Oct.-Nov.	3 lbs. = 3 cups cooked, mashed. Bright colored, unblemished, firm.	Room temperature 1 month or in refrigerator 1-4 months.	Halve, remove seeds and stringy portion. Bake or peel and cut into small pieces for steaming.
Radishes	Year round Peak: Apr.-July	Smooth, firm, well formed. Slight pressure will reveal undesirable spongy radishes.	Remove tops. Store in plastic bag in refrigerator 1-2 weeks.	Wash thoroughly, remove roots and damaged leaves.
Sweet Potato	Year round Peak: Sept.-Dec. Low: May-July	Smooth, well shaped, firm and bright. Dry type—mealy, light yellow tan. Moist type—white tan to brown red (often called yams).	Keep at room temperature several days. A closed box or plastic bag prevents wilting or drying out.	Scrub, do not peel.
Tomato	Yearly Low: winter months	Firm, plump, smooth, good color with no serious blemishes or cracks. Vine ripened.	If not fully ripened store at room temperature out of direct sunlight. Store ripe tomatoes uncovered in refrigerator 2-3 days.	Wash. Remove core with knife before quartering.
White Turnips	All year Peak: fall	2 lbs. for 4 servings. With fresh green tops, smooth and firm with some root attached. Heavy for size.	In vegetable crisper or plastic bag in refrigerator, 1 month.	Scrub, trim ends, and peel as thinly as possible.

COOKING VEGETABLES

Vegetables in the raw state have the highest nutritional value. Ideally most fruits and vegetables should be eaten uncooked. The vitamin loss increases with cooking time and increased amounts of cooking liquid. Vitamin C is also lost by long exposure to air. More nutrients are retained if the vegetable is cooked in its peel. If the peel itself is edible it is often very high in nutrients. The more cut surfaces you have, the easier for vitamins to be lost, so larger pieces are best for nutrition. Covering the cooking vegetables does not effect nutritional value since vitamins and minerals are not volatile and will not evaporate with the steam. Green vegetables will have a brighter color if cooked without a cover. However, if cooking time or the amount of liquid needed to prevent scorching must be increased significantly to cook the vegetable uncovered, it is inadvisable.

Specific directions are given in each recipe for cooking the vegetables. The following points should be kept in mind, however, for best results:

1. Cook whenever possible without water.

2. If you use water, use only enough to keep vegetables from sticking, or, where indicated, just enough to cover.

3. Cook leafy vegetables in only the water that clings to them after washing.

4. Bring water to a boil before adding vegetables. Cook gently over medium flame to prevent rapid evaporation of liquid and scorching.

5. Tender young vegetables, such as peas and carrots, can be cooked in butter with rinsed lettuce leaves placed over them in a pan with a tight-fitting lid.

6. Cook vegetables until just tender. Remove them immediately from hot liquid.

7. Never use baking soda to keep vegetables green. It destroys important minerals and vitamins A and B.

8. Cook vegetables that are to be served hot just before serving.

9. Use cooking liquid in sauces and soup stocks.

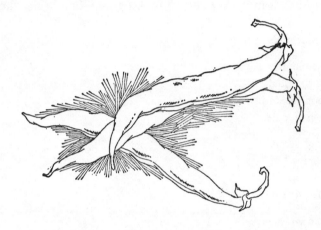

KITCHEN STAPLES

Here is a list of foods you will want to keep on hand for everyday cooking and eating, guaranteed to keep you from going hungry.

Raw Materials

　　whole wheat flour
　　corn meal
　　potato starch flour
　　rolled oats

　　raw sugar
　　honey
　　molasses
　　maple syrup

　　brown rice
　　buckwheat groats (kasha)
　　cracked wheat (bulghur)
　　whole wheat noodles
　　macaroni shells

　　assorted dried beans

　　raisins
　　assorted dried fruits
　　nuts
　　pine nuts
　　sesame seeds
　　peanut butter
　　wheat germ

sea salt or kosher salt
small quantities of dried herbs and spices
vegetable bouillon
Tamari soy sauce
vinegar
vegetable or nut oil
garlic

non-aluminum baking powder
baking soda
baker's yeast

cheese
butter
milk
eggs (have some hard-cooked on hand at all times)

tea
dry milk powder

cereals (for serving hot and cold)
whole wheat crackers or rye crackers
whole wheat graham crackers

pure jam, jelly, or preserves

apple juice (unsweetened, no preservatives) or cider
tomato juice

assorted fruits, including oranges for juicing
lemons
assorted raw vegetables

Prepared Foods

homemade or safflower oil mayonnaise
tomato sauce, frozen in 1-pint plastic containers
a loaf or two of homemade bread, rolls, and biscuits, frozen

FOOD EQUIVALENTS

DRIED BEANS

In general dried beans yield 2 to 3 times more when cooked. One pound serves 8 to 9.

1 pound	cups uncooked	cups cooked
white beans	2	6
kidney beans	2½	6¼
lima beans	3	7
soy beans	2¼	
lentils	2¼	5½
split peas	2	5
chick peas	2	5½

PASTA

Allow ¾ to 1 pound for 4 servings.

8 ounces	cups uncooked	cups cooked
macaroni	2	4
noodles	2¼	4
spaghetti	2½	4 to 5

Corn Meal: 1 pound=3 cups
1 cup uncooked=4 cups cooked
Brown Rice: 1 pound=2 cups raw=6 cups cooked

FLOUR

1 pound
  white flour=4 cups sifted
  whole wheat=3½ cups
  rolled oats=4¾ cups
  rye, light=5 cups
  rye, dark=3⅓ cups

DAIRY PRODUCTS

butter: ¼ pound (1 stick)=½ cup
    1 ounce=2 tablespoons
eggs: 4 to 6 whole=1 cup
    8 to 10 whites=1 cup
    12 to 16 yolks=1 cup
cheese: 1 pound (16 ounces)=4 cups grated
    (1 pound Parmesan grated=5 cups)
cottage cheese: 1 pound=2 cups
dry milk: 1 pound=4 cups

NUTS

1 pound in shell   *cups shelled*
    almonds   1½
    pecans   2¼
    walnuts   2
    peanuts   2 to 2½
1 pound shelled nuts=about 4 cups

FRUITS AND VEGETABLES

apples: 1 pound=3 medium=3½ cups sliced
bananas: 1 pound=3 to 4=2 cups mashed
lemons: 1 medium=2 to 3 tablespoons juice and 2 teaspoons rind

mushrooms: ½ pound=2½ cups sliced
oranges: 1 medium=⅓ cup juice and 2 tablespoons rind
onions: 1 medium=½ cup chopped
peas: 1 pound in shell=1 cup shelled
potatoes, white: 1 pound=3 medium=2½ cups diced=2 cups
  mashed
potatoes, sweet: 1 pound=1⅓ cups mashed
raisins: 1 pound=3 cups
tomatoes: 1 pound=3 medium=1 cup pulp

MISCELLANEOUS

garlic: 1 clove=¼ teaspoon chopped
bread: 1 slice=⅓ cup crumbs
graham crackers: 15=1 cup crumbs
dry yeast: 1 package=1 tablespoon

INGREDIENT SUBSTITUTIONS

FLOUR

For baking:

1 cup white flour=¾ cup whole wheat flour
                   1 cup corn flour or fine meal
                   ¾ cup coarse corn meal
                   ⅞ cup rice flour
                   1½ cups rye flour
                   ⅝ cup potato flour
                   1½ cups ground rolled oats
                   ½ cup barley flour

Adjustments may be needed in amount of liquid (usually more will be needed) and shortening (usually less is needed) when baking with whole grains.

For thickening sauces and other dishes:

1 tablespoon white flour=1 tablespoon whole wheat flour
                            1 tablespoon rice flour
                            1 tablespoon corn flour
                            ½ tablespoon corn starch
                            ½ tablespoon potato flour or starch
                            ½ tablespoon arrowroot

DAIRY PRODUCTS

1 cup milk=3 tablespoons dry milk powder plus 1 cup water
                 1 cup soy milk
                 1 cup fruit juice

1 cup sour milk or buttermilk=1 cup milk plus 1 tablespoon lemon juice or vinegar. Let stand 5 minutes.

1 cup butter=⅞ cup nut or vegetable oil

HERBS AND SPICES

½ teaspoon dried=about 1 tablespoon fresh herbs
⅛ teaspoon powdered ginger=1 tablespoon raw

SWEETENERS

For baking:

1 cup sugar=1 cup molasses+¼ to ½ teaspoon baking soda (omit baking powder)
=1 cup honey (reduce liquid ¼ cup)
=¾ cup maple syrup (reduce liquid 2 tablespoons)

Index

INDEX